Moving To Las Vegas

Moving to

Las Vegas

Third Edition

John L. Smith
& Patricia Smith

B a r r i c a d e   B o o k s   I n c .
Fort Lee, New Jersey

Published by Barricade Books Inc.
185 Bridge Plaza North, Suite 308-A
Fort Lee, NJ 07024
www.barricadebooks.com

Printed in Canada

Book design and page layout by CompuDesign.

Library of Congress Cataloging-in-Publication Data

Smith, John L., 1960–
    Moving to Las Vegas / John L. Smith and Patricia Smith.–
    3rd ed.
        p. cm.
    Rev. ed. of: Moving to Las Vegas / Theresa A. Mataga and
    John L. Smith. c1997.
    Includes index
    ISBN 1-56980-242-4
    1. Las Vegas (Nev.)–Description and travel. 2. Moving,
    Household–Nevada–Las Vegas. 3. Las Vegas (Nev.)–
    Guidebooks. I. Smith, Patricia. II Mataga, Theresa A.
    Moving to Las Vegas. III. Title.

F849.L35 S585 2002
979.3'135–dc21   2002026064

First Printing of Third Edition

Table of Contents

Acknowledgments

Although I am rarely shy about taking credit for such things, the idea for *Moving to Las Vegas* was not mine. It belongs to Theresa Mataga, who was the co-author of this book's first two editions. Theresa, a relative newcomer to Southern Nevada, contacted Lyle Stuart in 1996 with a proposal to write a book that would give the 5,000-and-more newcomers who moved to Las Vegas each month a brief, no-nonsense guide to making a successful life here. Lyle, who as a high-rolling gambler had his own 40-year relationship with Las Vegas, put Theresa and me together with positive results.

Now Theresa has passed the writing and researching baton to my wife, Tricia Smith. The new, expanded *Moving to Las Vegas* is approximately twice the size of previous editions. I'd like to think it is a lot like the city it chronicles, a work in progress that gets better with time. Meanwhile, Theresa's voice and views will be found in the Active Seniors chapter and it is to her that this new edition is dedicated. Here's to you, Theresa, and to the newcomers who call Las Vegas home.

Special thanks are due to graphic artist and computer wizard Mike Johnson of the *Las Vegas Review-Journal* for creating the maps for this edition. Thanks are also due to creators of the annual "Las Vegas Perspective" publication for compiling statistics. Statisticians with the state Gaming Control Board also deserve credit, as do several reporters from the *Las Vegas Review-Journal* by name: Dave Berns, Jan Moller, Frank Geary, Natalie Patton, Lisa Kim Bach, Glenn Puit, John G. Edwards, Jeff Simpson, and Hubble Smith.

Finally, thanks to our beautiful daughter, Amelia, who kept smiling despite our long stretches at the computer while working on this project.

Here's to the best future for all our children.

Introduction

A New World

It has often been said that the events of September 11, 2001 changed America forever. Outside New York and the Pentagon, perhaps no place in the country was affected more immediately than Las Vegas. Within hours after the first jet slammed into the World Trade Center, flights to tourist-dependent Las Vegas ceased when all commercial airline travel was grounded.

In less than a week, as the nation watched in shock as world events unfolded and President George W. Bush declared a war on terrorism, Nevada's essential and all-powerful gaming resort industry responded to the sudden economic slump by laying off approximately 30,000 employees. Many lost not only their jobs, but their health care as well. Lower Manhattan was burning, but the metaphorical smoke from that awful act of terrorism filled the air above the Strip. For Las Vegas, it was a rare event: a dramatic downturn in the economy.

While casino operators were vilified for their hair-trigger response—thousands of the layoffs came early and some of the terminations appeared to victimize older workers who had built seniority and who were more likely to use the company medical insurance—the decisions were made with an eye on the bottom line of the publicly-traded companies. When the criticism grew, executives at some properties decided to shed some of the heat by accepting sizable pay cuts as a show of support for the waiters, maids, and card dealers who'd lost their livelihood almost overnight with little prospect of returning to work before the end of 2001. Management decisions had another odd effect: the mass terminations actually moved Culinary Union officials, whose Local 226 is the largest labor organization in Las Vegas with more than 40,000 casino service workers as members, to briefly criticize casino executives. Such is life in this company town of approximately 1.4 million.

By spring 2002, resorts slowly began rehiring employees. It appeared the worst was over. But it became clear to many observers that the mass terminations had served more than one purpose for the industry. Reports from throughout Southern Nevada raised suspicion about the possible motives behind some of the layoffs. Cocktail waitresses complained that, despite their seniority, they were not rehired because they had committed the unpardonable sins of their trade: getting older and gain-ing a little weight. Their suspicions aside, the industry could point with justification to the dramatic decline in profits after September 11. Profits that began a return to normalcy before Christmas.

These are just a few of the issues facing Southern Nevada in this somewhat shaky new world. Beyond the immediate layoffs and the eventual return to normalcy, questions have been posed by Wall Street about the short-term growth potential for the resort industry in Las Vegas.

Following the greatest hotel room expansion in the nation's history, there was bound to be a lull in construction—and approximately one-third of Southern Nevada's booming economy was based on the presence of a lusty building market. But it's now clear that September 11 exacerbated that time out and raised issues of the practicality of funding multi-billion-dollar projects in a time of uncertainty and unprecedented proliferation of legalized gambling in other states, overseas, and on the Internet. What had been considered a consummately safe bet only a few years earlier has at least for the time being become a hard sell on Wall Street.

Only former Mirage Resorts Chairman Steve Wynn has announced his elaborate plans to build a new, $1.6 billion megaresort on the site of the venerable Desert Inn hotel, casino and country club. But as of early 2002 questions were still being raised in the press about the viability of Wynn's financing for his "Le Reve" project. Although some in the lending community shied away from Wynn after his controversial stewardship of Mirage Resorts, a company known for pampering its executives as well as catering to its high rollers, it seems inconceivable to most that the dynamic showman would somehow be unable to wow potential investors. Nevertheless, media reports continued to surface that Wynn might receive financial backing only with "substantial strings" attached. Surely his position in the market was bolstered after he won a coveted license to operate a casino on the island of Macau, gambling headquarters of the Far East. Beyond Le Reve, there were plenty of resort expansions in the works, including a massive convention center on property owned by Mandalay Resort Group, but the prospects for major new megaresorts being built in the near future seemed remote. The great wave of casino construction hadn't crashed, but it had broken.

Yet, the overall picture in Southern Nevada is anything but bleak. Las Vegas remains a national leader in a remarkable number of positive economic indicators. From housing and apartment construction to business start-ups and, yes, even job creation, it remains America's boomtown.

It has always been our goal to tell the Las Vegas story in an accurate and unvarnished manner. Warts and all, as it were. Newcomers to Las Vegas sooner or later realize that the community has been built largely on the masterful hype of its promoters, men who accentuated the glamour, bright lights, and hedonistic intrigue in order to attract throngs of gamblers and tourists. That self-promotion has worked marvelously well for decades, but it also has had the effect of deluding some people who move

here believing in that hype without clearly understanding that Southern Nevada is a rapidly growing,
culturally diverse, and complex community with
many attributes but plenty of growing pains of its
own.

With this new edition, we endeavor to continue
cutting through the fog and hype of the Great Las
Vegas Image Machine to give you the true sense of
what it is like to live, work, and raise a family in
America's most incredible boomtown. We are fond
of Las Vegas, blemishes and all, and it is with a sense
of caring that we promise to continue to tell it like
it is.

* * *

When you move to Las Vegas, you can expect
certain questions from outsiders. A popular one is,
"Do people actually live there?"

Sooner or later, you will be forced to explain
that, yes, you do live there and, no, you don't get
your mail at a Strip hotel.

"Is there a blackjack system that works?" is
another favorite. The answer is yes, but only if you
own a casino.

In recent years, by far the most often asked
question goes something like, "Las Vegas is booming now, but how long can it last?" It's a fair question, one that my family has been asking about
Nevada and Las Vegas since 1881. My ancestors
were among those early arrivals who believed it
wouldn't last, or at least I must presume that's so,
for we never bothered to buy land. I sometimes
imagine my great-great-grandparents standing at

the dusty roadside of progress with arms crossed and scowls firmly fixed, thinking, "Damn fools. Don't they know this will never last?"

And they were often right, at least as it concerned the gold- and silver-mining districts of Tonopah and Goldfield in central Nevada. If history is any indicator, Las Vegas differs from those played out mother lodes in one important regard: Its gold mines never close, and—here's the best part—the miners actually dump their own hard-earned ore into the claims.

That's the wonder of an economy based on casinos and tourism, and that's why answering the question is tougher than it seems.

Clark County has doubled and sometimes tripled in population each decade since its incorporation in 1905. Accompanying that tremendous growth and prosperity are some very real problems that residents must deal with each day.

From traffic and crime rates to the city's destructive lifestyle traditions, Las Vegas isn't simply some green-felt utopia on the Mojave desert. Yet it endures and prospers as never before. If its soul is troubled, it also is a place for second chances.

Las Vegas is the fastest-growing community in America. In a slow month, approximately four thousand people arrive with their dreams and goals and big ideas. For some, Las Vegas represents a chance at economic redemption after a lost job in hometowns across the nation. For others, it's a dream factory where on a given weekend they, too, might strike it rich. It's a foolish but seductive dream. Still others are making Las Vegas their retirement home and are taking advantage of the climate and the state's friendly tax structure.

I hope this book answers a few questions about this most amazing city.

—John L. Smith

1

The Golden Promise

Now that you have decided to live in Las Vegas, you should know something about its history. That's not as easy as it seems, for in Las Vegas, facts blend with legend the way a blackjack dealer shuffles a deck.

Hollywood lore would have you believe that the town was born when New York gangster Benjamin Siegel arrived in the early 1940s, but he was more than a century late in discovering this superheated spot in the Mojave Desert that has long held the promise of riches.

As a mark on a map, this place was first encountered by Spanish explorers in 1829. Before then, of course, there were the Paiute and Anasazi Indians.

Moving toward the coast in search of gold and trade routes, the Spaniards encountered a marshy desert oasis dotted with streams and artesian springs. They named it Las Vegas, or "the Meadows."

By 1843, U.S. Army officer John C. Fremont led a caravan through the region. For a time, poorly researched histories of the area falsely credited Fremont with discovering Las Vegas.

Next in line were Mormon missionaries, who arrived in 1855 and toiled with the devotion of true believers to carve out a civilization in the desert. They planted gardens and built walls and lasted two years before the climate, living conditions, and unfriendly Paiutes drove them back to Salt Lake City.

With an abundance of water and the region's first mail route, by Nevada's 1864 statehood, Las Vegas station was a stopping-off point for travelers making the long journey from Denver or Salt Lake City out to California.

It was water that attracted Montana Senator William Clark to the southern tip of Nevada when he and a group of investors determined to build the San Pedro, Los Angeles, and Salt Lake Railroad. Clark was the first of many big-spending, big-idea men envisioning big things for vast, empty Southern Nevada. By the time the tracks crossed the long valley in 1902, the area was inhabited by hearty ranchers, foraging Indians, and poisonous snakes. Las Vegas never was an easy place to live.

Traveling card sharks used rest stops at Las Vegas to take advantage of suckers and simpletons, and the first tent gambling parlors were born. By the time Las Vegas officially took its name in 1905, it already had its share of gamblers and easy women. Some say that not much has changed in those almost one hundred years.

Four years later, growing out from the railroad tracks, Las Vegas sported six hotels, a single hardware store, and eleven saloons and brothels at Block 16, the founding fathers' testament to the power and profit of vice. Clark's railroad may have put Las Vegas on the map, but Block 16's Arizona Club and Black Cat Club would define its image for decades to come. Although the townsfolk frowned on dice-dealing and carousing, most benefitted by the dollars such activities generated.

Another marvelous myth about Las Vegas is that gambling always has been legal here. Far from it. It was, in fact, illegal but tolerated for much of the early twentieth century. Legalization came in 1931. Not only would the tax revenue generated feed the state's depleted coffers in the early years of the Great Depression, but touting legal casino games was sure to attract the hundreds of workers building Hoover Dam. With gambling illegal in Boulder City near the dam site, the construction stiffs made frequent trips to Las Vegas and Searchlight, where cold beer, hot cards, and willing women were available for a price.

More than 100 years had passed since Fremont drew his map, and there was still no sign of Bugsy Siegel. A decade after legalization, the city had become well-known to racketeers hungry to stretch their legs without fear of law enforcement intervention. The El Rancho Vegas was built south of downtown along U.S. Highway 91, and the Hotel Last Frontier with its entertaining jingle, "the Early West in Modern Splendor," appeared a year later.

By then, Siegel had been spotted in Las Vegas. A founding member of New York's Bug and Meyer mob, Siegel was sent west by his partner, Meyer Lansky, to avoid a murder rap and cinch up the syndicate's horse-wire interests. It was a mission Siegel welcomed, for he fancied himself as movie star potential (he even had a screen test), courted starlets, and loved to pal around with childhood-friend-turned-screen-gangster, George Raft. His fantasy aside, Siegel was an egotistical hood prone to fits of extreme violence.

He also wasn't shy about making offers other men couldn't refuse. When *Hollywood Reporter* founder and original Flamingo developer Billy Wilkerson ran short of cash, Siegel was there to infuse thousands into the project. Siegel, Lansky, and other East Coast mob bosses already owned pieces of the Golden Nugget and El Cortez downtown, and the Flamingo held the promise of a syndicate desert palace. In a matter of months, Siegel's investment ballooned to more than $1 million, but he had even bigger plans for the resort.

It would have riding stables, tennis courts, mature shrubs, and trees. It would feature a swimming pool, opulent rooms, and a fourth-floor suite devoted entirely to himself. And the costs kept climbing.

Siegel's $1 million investment of the mob's money in the Flamingo was a fiasco of the first order. Between theft on the job site and the high prices of construction materials in the months following the end of World War II, he had set himself up as a patsy as costs climbed toward $6 million. To make matters worse, inclement weather and lucky gamblers made the Flamingo's December 1946 opening a financial flop. The casino closed for a short time, then reopened in the spring of 1947 and immediately began making money.

But it was too late for Siegel. His friends had decided that his lack of business acumen would cost him his life. On June 20, 1947, Siegel was murdered at the Beverly Hills home of his gun-moll girlfriend, Virginia Hill.

Siegel's name burned in the psyche of the mob-loving American public. Whenever Las Vegas was mentioned, the infamous Bugsy was sure to be nearby.

Other men have had a far greater impact on Las Vegas than Siegel, but few compare to the quiet craftsmanship of quintessential racketeer-turned-businessman Morris "Moe" Dalitz. Born in Boston in 1899, Dalitz ran rackets in Detroit, Cleveland, and Newport, Kentucky, before joining the western migration of illegal gamblers to the land of the legitimate dice game. Using their friend Wilbur Clark as a front, Dalitz and his Cleveland partners built the Desert Inn in 1950. Using his contacts with Jimmy Hoffa's Teamsters Central States Pension Fund, Dalitz arranged for the purchase and construction of numerous other hotels. To his great credit, he diversified his business interests to include the construction of the first for-profit hospital in southern Nevada, the first large shopping mall, the first successful private golf course, and some of the most successful housing developments in the city's history. Dalitz, who had thrived in a violent racket, died of natural causes at age eighty-nine.

The history of Las Vegas is the story of the influence of many men and one woman, Lady Luck.

There was nutty billionaire Howard Hughes, who arrived by train at night on Thanksgiving 1966. Hughes purchased seven casinos and vast tracts of real estate and was credited, falsely, with ridding the city of the mob by infusing his so-called clean capital. Although much of the media bought the ruse, Hughes was at best an eccentric landlord who in reality built not a single hotel or casino on the Strip. His greatest contribution in our opinion was his obsessive acquisition of thousands of acres of raw real estate at the farthest northern and western edges of the community. That acreage is now the site of the impressive Summerlin community.

Of greater importance in terms of casino development is Kirk Kerkorian, the Los Angeles native who grew a multibillion-dollar empire from the sales of airplane and aircraft parts in the years after World War II. On his way to becoming a Las Vegas legend, Kerkorian built the world's largest hotel three times (the International in 1969, the MGM Grand in 1973, and the MGM Grand Hotel and Theme Park in 1994).

Other influences include the wildly imaginative Jay Sarno, who dreamed up the themes for Caesars Palace and Circus Circus and had his sights set on building a behemoth 6,000-room megaresort years before anyone dared to dream that big. Today, the 5,005-room MGM Grand makes Sarno look like a visionary.

If Las Vegas had an undisputed king in the 1990s, it was Steve Wynn. As chairman of Mirage Resorts, Wynn was responsible for employing nearly 20,000 workers. His creativity has shone through with a man-made volcano at the Mirage and a life-size pirate battle at Treasure Island. Wynn also exercised considerable political will at the local, state, and national levels and became the living symbol of legalized gaming in corporate America.

In 1998, Mirage Resorts opened the posh Bellagio resort on the former site of the Dunes Hotel. With its multimillion-dollar works of art, Wynn believed Bellagio would signal continued prosperity for Las Vegas and would remake the city as a playground for the world's well-heeled traveler. He was wrong. Wynn's extravagant resort and even more liberal use of shareholder investment dollars led to a plummeting of Mirage stock and the acquisition of the company in 2000 by Kerkorian's MGM Grand. The company is now called MGM Mirage, and Wynn is in the process of regrouping with the development of the Desert Inn property under a project called "Le Reve."

Las Vegas will continue to prosper economically as long as the gambling industry continues to expand. That economic prosperity, however, has not translated into smart planning on the part of the community's power brokers and politicians. The need for smart planning and fast action have never been more urgent.

Prior to World War II, a local political structure barely existed. The first attempt at Las Vegas-style comprehensive planning occurred in 1953 when county officials created a land use guide. The city followed suit in 1959 with the General Master Plan. Everything from annexation and land use to the water supply and sewer system was addressed. And promptly forgotten. Southern Nevada's developers and casino men were too busy growing and making money to worry about planning.

Nearly 40 years would pass before the county's so-called Smart Growth Program would signal an era in which planned growth was beginning to be taken seriously. By then, the image of Las Vegas as a growth center had started to suffer under the weight of fears of too little water, a rapidly decreasing quality of air and a diminished quality of life for residents. Casino men and even some developers jumped on the slow-growth bandwagon.

The Las Vegas Valley Water District is in the process of constructing a second pipeline from Lake Mead in order to better serve customers. Key state legislators such as Sen. Dina Titus have played a big role in forcing the growth agenda, not only at the state but also at the local levels. Titus and others have advocated setting specific growth boundaries within the Las Vegas Valley similar to the plan in use in Portland, Oregon. The "Ring Around the Valley" idea was controversial in growth-crazed Las Vegas, but Titus has vowed to continue fighting to curtail unchecked development.

Growth and development on the Strip became such a hot issue in early 1999 that MGM Grand President J. Terrence Lanni, one of the most respected men in the casino business, publicly suggested a moratorium on new hotel rooms unless planned megaresorts removed older rooms from the city's burgeoning balance. With 126,000 hotel rooms expected to be available before the turn of the century, Lanni's concern appeared justified. "There's going to be a capacity problem, there's no doubt about that," Lanni said.

As with all things in Las Vegas, the bottom line is what the top members of the powerful casino industry think. It was ever thus, and ever thus will be. Whether you believe the old gamblers got out or simply grew up doesn't matter, really. Today, Las Vegas is as legitimately corporate as any place in America. And it prospers as never before, thanks to the continued explosion of growth in the casino districts and throughout the valley.

Las Vegas exists almost as much in the eye of the American psyche as on any map. As a city, it defines the present. It is electric and illusory, shallow and symbolic. With its notorious past, its city fathers bury its history in fable and public relations.

Gazing down the Las Vegas Strip with its bright lights, wild architecture, and high-rise megaresorts, it's hard to imagine a time when the only nighttime illumination available was that from the moon.

But the world has discovered Las Vegas. It is a resort destination city, a gambling mecca, an entertainment capital.

It also is a place where approximately 1.5 million people live and work and raise their families. Far from a vision of fantasy, the reality of Las Vegas is that it is an enormously prosperous factory town with enormous potential and sizable challenges.

Now that you're here, it's time to call it home.

2

Sketching the Vegas Profile

You're a forty-seven-year-old white woman, married, and you own your own home. You come from California, have lived in Las Vegas less than five years, and came here for the economic opportunities, tax structure, and mild winters. You've had some college and recently have changed your political party affiliation from Democrat to Republican.

And one more thing.

You are a demographer's dream.

In short, that is the profile of the average Las Vegan: statistically generated, of course, for the booming southern Nevada population is anything but typical.

Fact is, Las Vegas gets a little more gray each year. (This, no doubt, will come as a relief to those of you planning to make it your permanent home.) Poet Robert Browning came up with the ideal Las Vegas motto when he wrote, "Grow old along with me, the best is yet to be," and that appears to apply to southern Nevada as well. At least, statistically.

In 1980, the median age of the typical Las Vegan was 40.1 years. Throw in the kids, and the average dipped to 29.7. By 1985, as the valley's senior retirement centers began to catch on with retirees from across the nation, the average age increased to 32.5 with children included. By 1995, the average age of the adult population was 47.

Although the vast majority of southern Nevada's one million residents is white, 75.4 percent according to the 1990 Census, the population remains diverse. One in nine Las Vegans is Hispanic, one in eleven African American, one in thirty Asian. Of all ethnic groups, the Hispanic population has grown the most in the past decade, increasing from 8 percent of the population to 11.2 percent.

Nearly six in ten households have two adults. Almost seven in ten have no children. Although 29 percent of southern Nevadans have maintained residency more than twenty years, more than half the population has been in the valley a decade.

Now comes the staggering part: 7.3 percent of the population, or about one in fourteen southern Nevadans, has lived in Las Vegas less than a year. That's a boomtown by anyone's measure, but at least you need not feel like the only new kid on the block. Not with the community's expansion and projected growth. In July 1996 alone, 6,620 people made Las Vegas their new residence.

In 1945, about the time Bugsy Siegel got his bright idea to come out to Las Vegas, Clark County's population was 20,000, including jackass prospectors and sand-and-sage cattle ranchers. On the way to surpassing the one million mark, Las Vegas reached the 500,000 mark in the early 1980s, hitting 552,900 by 1985.

That means this diverse population doubled in a decade.

It also has spread out from old and new cities of Henderson (the new Henderson goes by the name Green Valley) on the southeast side of the valley to Mesquite near the Nevada-Utah border. Mesquite, for example, is rapidly transforming itself from a ranching community to one of the hottest casino border towns in the country. Although its population, at just more than 5,500, is tiny by some standards, it represents a 58 percent growth in a single year.

Henderson, once a smoky World War II industrial site, has grown into Nevada's third-largest city with a 1995 population figure of nearly 120,000.

The only spot in southern Nevada that has resisted growth is Boulder City, which emerged during the building of Hoover Dam in the early years of the Great Depression and does not allow casino gambling inside the city limits. With 14,100 residents and located just fourteen miles from downtown, it is one of the places Las Vegans go to get away from other Las Vegans.

Where are all the people coming from?

California, for starters. A full 42 percent of Las Vegas newcomers hail from the Golden State, which threatened to be renamed the gold-plated state after its oppressive tax structure and early 1990s real estate crash sent thousands fleeing to other states. Southern Nevada also is home to equal measures of New Yorkers and Texans, who some locals believe serve to cancel each other out. Actually, 17 percent of newcomers arrive from the Northeast and Southwest. Another 9.5 percent come from the Midwest, 9 percent from the South. Just more than 5 percent of new residents are from the Northwest.

The state-by-state breakdown, according to the Department of Motor Vehicles, goes something like this: California, Arizona, New York, Texas, Florida, Illinois, Colorado, Utah, Michigan, and Washington.

Nearly three of four southern Nevadans are registered to vote. Traditionally, a majority of the valley's residents was a registered Democrat. That has changed in recent years. In 1995, 42.6 percent of those registered had done so as Republicans, slightly more than the 39.1 percent of registered Democrats. Both Nevada's senators, Harry Reid and Richard Bryan, are Democrats, and as of Election Year 1998, both of the state's members of the House of Representatives, Barbara Vucanovich and John Ensign, were Republicans.

More than other states, Nevada's political history is decidedly Libertarian and, some would argue, libertine as well. More than 18 percent of registered voters consider themselves Independent or members of a less traditional political party.

Once you have begun to comprehend the rate of growth, it's a little easier to appreciate the challenges faced by community planners who went to sleep in a bustling desert outpost and awoke in America's last great boomtown. It might not keep your automobile from overheating while you're sweating out a rush-hour traffic jam or keep you from overheating while waiting for hours to change your license plates at the Department of Motor Vehicles, but at least you can understand what all the commotion is about.

By 1998, the valley's population had risen to 1.3 million, making Clark County the third fastest-growing county in the nation. According to state demographic experts, at the current rate of expansion—some 5,000 people per month moving to Las Vegas is expected to continue. By 2018, more than 2.7 million people will be crowded into the Las Vegas valley.

The December 1998 jobless rate, at 3.1 percent, was the lowest in 41 years. Not since 1957 had the state's unemployment rate been as low. In all, 46,500 new jobs were produced, thanks mostly to the opening of the Bellagio and the construction of other megaresorts in Las Vegas. Once you've moved to Las Vegas, you soon realize that the city is the economic engine that drives the state.

On the downside, Las Vegans smoke, drink and, not surprisingly, gamble more than citizens in other cities. The suicide rate is nearly twice the national average. It is a city of great promise and great falls.

And vocal enemies.

Dr. James Dobson, President and founder of the Focus on the Family nonprofit Christian organization, was a member of the National Gambling Impact Study Commission, which held meetings across America in 1998 to discuss the influence of legalized gambling on society. In a January 1999 letter to his followers, Dobson attacked legalized gambling and, in effect, Las Vegas, as never before.

"But what about the glitz and glamour of Nevada?" Dobson wrote. "If one scratches beneath the veneer of its gambling-induced prosperity, it becomes apparent that a culture sown on greed and the exploitation of human weakness invariably reaps the social whirlwind. Consider these documented facts: When compared with the 49 other states, Nevada ranks first in the nation in suicide, first in divorce, first in high school dropouts, first in homicide against women, at the top of gambling addictions, third in bankruptcies, third in abortion, fourth in rape, fourth in out-of-wedlock births, fourth in alcohol-related deaths, fifth in crime, and sixth in the number of prisoners locked up. It also ranks in the top one-third of the nation in child abuse, and dead-last in voter participation. One-tenth of all southern Nevadans are alcoholics. And as for the moral climate, the Yellow Pages of Las Vegas lists 136 pages of advertisements for prostitution by its various names. No wonder they call it 'Sin City.'"

There's something else you should know about moving to Las Vegas. You must be sure to bring with you a thick skin. For all its growth and economic prosperity, and the many positive aspects of living in southern Nevada, it's likely the name will forever be stigmatized simply as a den of sin and degradation.

Things change so quickly in Las Vegas that Sprint Telephone of Nevada must publish a telephone directory twice per year. This directory includes simple city maps, information on cultural and recreational activities, and calendars for many civic organizations.

Once you have moved to Las Vegas, you will wonder at what point you get to call yourself a local. After you have changed your auto license plates, you will be difficult to distinguish from the next newcomer. Here's something to remember: only 22 percent of Las Vegas residents were born in the valley. That means most of the people you meet are a lot like you—from somewhere else.

Chances are good there's room for you in southern Nevada even if you don't fit the profile.

3

Getting Around Town

The winding weekend pilgrimage of tourists from Southern California to Las Vegas on Interstate 15 surely is one of the most incredible spectacles in the history of the automobile. Whether you have lived in Las Vegas a generation or an hour, there is something awe inspiring, and a little scary, about the river of headlamps and metal streaking toward Las Vegas at high rates of speed. The river stretches out for miles northbound on I-15 on Friday night, then reverses itself come Sunday morning. Despite all the marketing and expansion that has taken place in the city in recent years, Las Vegas still draws its largest percentage of gamblers from Southern California.

In 1995, 4.28 million automobiles flowed through Yermo Inspection Station in San Bernardino County, California. The Las Vegas Convention and Visitors Authority uses the annual inspection station figures as a marketing barometer for Southern California. How the city is doing with San Diegans and Los Angelenos is measured in large part by how many vehicles pass the station. In a decade, vehicle traffic along Interstate 15 had increased from 2.68 million automobiles.

With that image in mind, you may ask yourself some superheated summer afternoon, "Why are they all trying to merge into my lane?"

Add to that the more than 30 million passengers flowing through McCarran International Airport each year, and you have the makings of a traffic jam anywhere in the city from tourist traffic alone.

As you can see, all roads lead to Las Vegas.

Like many American cities, Las Vegas has streets brimming with commuters riding one to a vehicle. One of the noticeable improvements in the transportation picture is the continued growth of the Citizens Area Transit bus system. The CAT carries approximately 4 million passengers each month. Of course, the single largest percentage of passengers, two of every ten, rides the Strip bus, which has been popular with tourists for decades. The CAT system is still stretching out in a community which is only beginning to form park-and-ride programs.

If part of your regular commute includes airline travel, it's important to note that McCarran

International Airport, one of the busiest airports in the world, offers 900 scheduled flights a day, and the number of passengers using the facility has doubled in the past decade. In 1998, McCarran opened a shiny new D Terminal with 26 new gates. With an 8.8-percent average annual growth rate over the past decade, McCarran is going to need each of those gates as it is projected to soon become one of the five busiest airports in the United States.

But most of you will spend a great deal of time in your cars on the roadways. As with most American cities, the largest traffic volumes are recorded during the morning and evening rush hours.

According to a UNLV study, peak hours on city streets generally correspond to 7 AM to 9 AM and 4 PM to 6 PM. McCarran Airport and Las Vegas Boulevard are always busy.

A 1998 UNLV traffic study concluded: "Infrastructure solutions will require improvements for both the tourist and local resident populations that visit and live in the Las Vegas valley. The lack of infrastructure will constrain the number of tourists who can travel to Las Vegas. This will undermine the success of the gaming industry as the supply of new resort hotels and casinos (Bellagio, Paris, Venetian, and Mandalay Bay) continues to increase. Also, the increasing congestion on local arterial and collector streets will degrade the quality of life experienced by local residents. This in turn will have a negative effect on the image of the Las Vegas Valley and its ability to attract new residents."

Meanwhile, transportation departments at the

various governmental entities continue to scramble to catch up.

At times it can seem as if each one of those roads is jammed bumper to bumper with seething drivers attempting to merge into your lane.

How you perceive southern Nevada's traffic and transportation issues once largely depended on where you came from. Those harried Los Angelenos like to scoff at locals who complain about expressway gridlock and the seemingly never-ending road projects that have become regular occurrences in Las Vegas. Newcomers from, say, Boise, are more likely to grouse that the daily traffic tie-ups, especially during the sweltering summer months, are almost too much to bear.

Today, all southern Nevadans have at least one thing in common. It's the traffic. With as many as 6,000 new residents per month, the streets of Las Vegas have been overwhelmed by automobiles. Commutes that only a few years ago took a matter of minutes to complete now take a half hour and longer.

Hold this truth close to your city map, wind-shield shade, and "I'm a local, what's it to ya?" bumper sticker: There will be no getting around the city's increasingly twisted traffic problems for the next several years. Help is on the way, but your Yugo is likely to turn 100,000 miles before all the lofty plans to relieve traffic congestion are set in asphalt.

How much traffic you feel you can endure will have a direct impact on where you purchase a home in the valley. Some of the spiffiest new neighbor-hoods in the far reaches of the valley are still only ten miles from the downtown business district, but average thirty minutes of driving time during rush hour. A one-hour daily commute might not make veterans of the Santa Ana Freeway break out in a cold sweat, but, given a five-day work week, it is nearly eleven whole days a year spent huffing diesel fumes and listening to inane radio talk show hosts.

Most knowledgeable students of the valley's traf-fic woes will tell you they were flat overwhelmed by the crush of automobiles. Extensive studies are ongoing. But here's how far off a previous Nevada Department of Transportation study was: In 1975, the agency predicted that by 1995, 48,500 vehicles would use a stretch of asphalt on U.S. 95 between Valley View and Rancho Drive. By 1995, they had missed their prediction by nearly 100,000 automo-biles. For the record, traffic is expected to increase from 1.02 million trips per day in 1995 to 1.79 mil-lion trips in 2015. Locals just hope the prediction isn't off by a factor of three.

From the most optimistic commuter to the most cynical cabdriver, and all the experts in between, no one anticipates traffic congestion easing in south-ern Nevada any time soon despite the millions of dollars in improvements underway. A few of the changes we can expect:

- Installing traffic signals at the on-ramps to U.S. 95.
- Converting U.S. 95 into a double-deck freeway with a four-lane connector to Interstate 15.

•. Widening U.S. 95 from the north end of the valley to Interstate 15, forcing dozens of residents to lose their homes.

Meanwhile, a valley-wide Las Vegas Beltway nears completion—at least as it's defined by county government. (When this book was first published in 1997, the I-215 beltway projection was still being negotiated.) In April 2002, the Clark County Commission voted not to make the Beltway actually circle the valley, instead opting not to take up to 1,000 homes at a cost of as much as $900 million in East Las Vegas. So, at least for the foreseeable future, the Beltway will be more like the Horseshoe. "To do this (an eastern beltway) is so incredibly expensive and so disruptive to the community, I think we need to be real about it," Commissioner Bruce Woodbury said in a *Review-Journal* story. "This is why we didn't pursue it originally." Even with the Beltway encircling only three-fourths of the valley, it's still 53 miles long and stretches from U.S. 95 in the southeast to Interstate 15 in the northeast.

If you have questions, the Nevada Department of Transportation is willing to listen. Visit their office at 7551 Sauer Drive, near the Rainbow Library at the corner of Buffalo and Cheyenne. But start early in case you get stuck in traffic.

Some of the ideas being considered include widening Interstate 15 to as many as 10 lanes; improving 50 streets; building a new mass transit center in North Las Vegas, and adding express bus routes.

With a rapidly increasing traffic flow and daily

tie-ups commonplace, sometimes it must seem as if Las Vegans can't get there from here. But they can, and the average commute to work in southern Nevada is approximately 20 minutes, about two minutes longer than the 1990 national average, according to the United States Census.

But here's the rub: Locals in newer parts of the valley now complain of bottlenecks before even reaching the newly widened freeways. At times, it takes as long to merge onto the expressway as it does to drive all the way across town. But that, too, is being addressed. It just takes time, and the great Las Vegas migration won't wait. How will you get from point A to point B? By the shortest route possible, of course.

Several options are available for those wishing to battle the urban sprawl.

CAT Bus

The Citizens Area Transit (CAT) bus system offers approximately forty routes throughout the Las Vegas valley and operates twenty hours each day. The Downtown Transportation Center is the transfer point for all CAT buses. Buses run every fifteen minutes for busy routes, every thirty minutes in peak hours, and every sixty minutes in non-peak hours. Fares are reasonable, and monthly passes are also available. CAT buses are accessible to people in wheelchairs and those needing help reaching the first step. Free certified personal-care attendants are available for customers with disabilities through the CAT Paratransit service.

The sprawling valley and the limited number of buses means that riders must sometimes walk considerable distances to reach a bus stop, and if you miss your bus, you often must wait an hour for the next one. Most routes are not direct, and often riders must wait additional time to transfer at the Downtown Transportation Center in order to get on the bus that will take them to their destination. For these inconveniences, residents consider using the bus system only as a last resort when a personal vehicle is not affordable.

For more information on the CAT bus system, call 228-7433.

Taxis

A dozen taxi companies operate in Las Vegas under the administration of the Taxi Cab Authority. All taxis charge the same fare.

With so many Vegas visitor calls on the Strip and downtown, it often is difficult to get a taxi to your home if you live too far outside the tourist areas of town. Taxi drivers prefer to stay near the easy-money areas, including McCarran International Airport. The only taxi companies that take credit cards (American Express only) are Yellow Cab, Checker Cab, and Star Cab.

Trolleys

The city operates eight rubber-wheeled trolleys on the Strip, from the Sahara Hotel to the Luxor Hotel. They run every twenty minutes and make stops at the front door of each major hotel on the route. Another trolley runs from the Downtown Transportation Center through downtown, to a supermarket and shopping center, and to the Howard Cannon Senior Center. This trolley is available Monday through Friday, 9 AM to 5 PM at twenty-minute intervals.

The last trolley line is the Meadows Mall express trolley, which runs Monday through Saturday, 10:30 AM to 5 PM. This trolley is a convenient way for people working downtown to go shopping on their lunch hour without having to worry about parking or driving.

Becoming Street Legal

When you move to Nevada, your out-of-state license can only be used for thirty days. You will need to go to one of the full-service branches of the Nevada Department of Motor Vehicles and Public Safety (DMV) to obtain a new license and register your vehicle.

To obtain your Nevada driver's license, you will need to bring proof of your name and age (birth certificate, out-of-state driver's license or passport) and proof of your Social Security number (Social Security card or payroll slip). You must pass a written test based on the driving laws of the state of Nevada. You can obtain a booklet at the DMV entitled, "Nevada Driver's Handbook," which covers all the information on the written test. There is a fee of $21.75 for a driver's license ($16.75 for seniors), which will be good for four years.

To register your vehicle in Nevada, you must have the following:

- Nevada Emission Control Certificate;
- Proof of liability insurance on the vehicle;
- Your current registration certificate;
- Verification of vehicle identification (which will be issued to you when your vehicle is inspected);
- Your out-of-state license plates.

To obtain a Nevada Emission Control Certificate, you must go to an authorized service station (on just about every corner; look for the signs) and ask for a smog test. Prices vary, so it pays to shop around before you choose a station. Your vehicle will be connected to a machine and a reading taken. If the vehicle passes, you will be issued a Nevada Emission Control Certificate. If the vehicle does not pass, you will be required to make repairs to your vehicle until it will pass the test.

Your vehicle must have liability insurance, and Nevada's insurance rates are among the highest in the country—not to mention that insurance companies can refuse to cover you if they don't like your credit record. Premiums will vary incredibly, so be sure to check around. Your rates will be best, of course, if you have no accidents or tickets on your record.

Your vehicle will be inspected for safety. They will check the lights, turn signals, horn, seat belts, speedometer, and muffler. Also be sure you have a gas cap on your gas tank.

The worst part of registration is the fee, which

in Nevada is actually a thinly disguised tax. The newer and more expensive your vehicle is, the more it will cost to register.

Call the DMV for information or visit the user-friendly website at www.dmvstat.com. Especially helpful on the website is the "new resident guide" on the main page which sets forth in great detail every possibility of what you may encounter in obtaining a new license and registration in Nevada. You will also find that reregistering and renewing your driver's license is a virtual snap and can be accomplished online.

Once you're street legal, you can join the thousands of other commuters who manage to navigate the streets of the boomtown each day without incident. As for improving the asphalt infrastructure, try to remain patient, and remember help is on the way. Unless it gets stuck in traffic.

4

Settling In

Not long after the tracks of William Clark's railroad crossed the valley, Las Vegas faced its first housing crisis. For visitors, accommodations were limited to a cramped room at Ladd's Hotel, where for one dollar travelers bought eight hours of sleep. But they were mistaken if they thought they also received privacy. Alas, room was so scarce, the beds had to be shared.

In those days, people planning to make a home in Las Vegas had to build their own. A lot has changed in ninety years.

Today, the Las Vegas valley is quickly filling up with scores of housing, condominium, and apartment developments. But, with thousands of people moving to the city each month, demand remains high. The traditional availability of large sections of raw desert real estate has proved one of the saving graces in the southern Nevada home market—and is a big reason for the sprawl issues that face the area. Although developments have wreaked havoc with the endangered desert tortoise, the little fellas were removed and relocated by government order, and they have been able to keep up with the growing demand for houses and apartments. Favorable interest rates have been a boon to the already booming market, and homebuyers have been known to camp out overnight at sales offices to take full advantage of developments in the more popular sections of the valley.

In 1995, the average price of a home in Las Vegas was $130,000. In July 1996, 1,594 new homes were sold and another 1,628 existing homes were resold. Those numbers compare favorably to cities three times the size of Las Vegas. If that sounds outrageous, remember that southern Nevada became home to 6,620 new residents in July alone. With an unemployment rate around 5.25 percent, and several years of growth still expected, it's no wonder the valley has become a magnet for people seeking second chances.

In September 1998, the median price of a new home was $136,600, according to Home Builders Research Inc. That's an 8 percent increase over the previous year. But that doesn't mean those selling homes were having a party. With about 20,000 new homes built in 1998, resale prices are some of the poorest in the country. Existing home prices rose a mere 2.2 percent in the year ending September 1998. That's the second worst percentage in the nation, ahead of only Hawaii. California led the nation with the average value of an existing home jumping 8.5 percent.

Southern Nevada continues to attract apartment development, but the signs are the boom in this market might be coming to an end. With more than 40,000 units built in the 1990s, there is a temporary glut. Monthly rates average $687, a slight decrease from 1997, when more than 10,000 units were built.

Las Vegas appears to have an abundance of all levels of housing—except the affordable kind as defined by the federal government. Demand far outstrips supply in this area.

To quote a 1998 UNLV housing study: "Affordable housing will continue to be a significant issue for Clark County as the area's population continues to grow. Housing costs in the Las Vegas valley continue to rise faster than increases in household income."

It is important to note that prices for homes of similar square footage and quality vary widely depending on location. In the popular northwest section of the valley, a three-bedroom, two-bath home can be purchased for approximately $170,000. Across the line dividing Las Vegas from North Las Vegas, only a couple miles from the heart of the northwest expansion, the price of a similar home is about $160,000. Further east, the price continues to drop into the $140,000 range.

Why the difference?

North Las Vegas has a largely undeserved reputation as a city stricken by a high crime rate. It is, in fact, no less safe than most Las Vegas neighborhoods. But it is a working-class town with a well-worn midsection, a fact which led city leaders to push for the release of thousands of acres of raw real estate closer to the northwest side from the Bureau of Land Management. The real estate was purchased by local developers, who have created something akin to the New North Las Vegas. A "Golden Triangle," as they like to call it.

Green Valley in the southeastern end of southern Nevada is a prime example of well-planned growth in a development boom largely ruled by chaos. Its thoroughfares are wide, its developments lined with grass and trees. Commercial development is generally more tightly controlled than in other parts of the valley, and in a valley lacking in parks and community cultural activities, Green Valley is a success story. With increased freeway access and the community-wide beltway passing nearby, it also makes increasing sense for commuters.

Although your first inclination is likely to be to search for a home in one of the sparkling new neighborhoods that seem to pop up daily, many of the best buys are found in the more established areas. You also get the benefit of mature trees and shrubs, and you will be able to enjoy the quality of life in a neighborhood free of that cookie-cutter feel.

Keep in mind your lifestyle, and make sure that what you need is close by. Las Vegas continues to suffer from a shortage of elementary, middle, and high schools. Find out where the nearest schools, hospitals, doctors, and shopping centers are, and most importantly, how far this home is from where you plan to work.

Now, a strong warning about homeowners' associations. They are quite common in the newer neighborhoods, especially in the planned communities of Green Valley, Spring Valley, Summerlin, Desert Shores, and Peccole Ranch. To be sure, living in a tightly controlled community has its advantages. The intricate list of Covenants, Conditions, and Restrictions has the effect of keeping neighborhoods uniform and maintaining property values. But the CC&R's also are a good way to have other people mind your business. They were designed to ensure uniformity and tranquillity in neighborhoods, but, depending on the nosiness of your particular neighbors and the personalities of the members of the board of the association, the rules can and often do result in Orwellian living conditions.

Liens are put on homes for downright silly code violations such as leaving your garage door open more than a foot, painting your house trim the wrong shade of an approved color, having a satellite dish, putting up a basketball stand, or having non-regulation shrubbery. One poor soul was harassed for daring to hang an American flag in his front yard. Long-fought lawsuits over the rights of homeowners have had inconsistent outcomes.

Association fees are also something to consider when buying in the newer, planned neighborhoods. Unlike your mortgage payment, association fees never go away and range anywhere from $20 to more than $200 per month depending on the neighborhood. And if you happen to get behind in your payment of association fees, the association has the legal right to put a lien on your home for any unpaid fees and proceed toward auctioning your home to the highest bidder.

If you're renting, you will be faced with the reality that the apartment market in Las Vegas is fast becoming an expensive way to go. Even studio and one-bedroom apartments rent for more than $600 a month in some areas, and the average price for a two-bedroom place continues to climb to more than $800. Given the low interest rates of the early 2000's, a monthly mortgage payment for a $140,000 starter home was no more than the price of renting a two-bedroom apartment. There are approximately 150,000 apartment units in the Las Vegas area. Discounts for seniors, military, and casino workers can be found in some apartments. Since Las Vegas has no rent-control laws, and demand is at a premium, rent hikes are common. Garbage collection and water fees are included in the rental price at most complexes. Most apartment-leasing companies require a six-month or one-year lease along with a security deposit of approximately $200. Expect to complete an application and credit report. If you are not employed, expect to show a bank statement to prove you will be able to pay the rent during the time of the lease.

If you rent a home, the usual procedure is to pay the first and last months' rent plus a security deposit—usually about $2,000 total. Be careful reading the contract; some owners are dishonest and may be able to retain your security deposit for no other reason than that they wish to. It might be well worth your money to pay an attorney for one hour of time to look over your paperwork. Make sure the contract explains exactly how your security deposit will be accounted for.

If you plan to purchase or rent a mobile home, a helpful publication is the free pamphlet, "Mobile Home Finder," found in entryways in many grocery stores.

Landscaping

Las Vegas's dry climate and shortage of water are two good reasons to consider a desert landscape for your home. The Las Vegas Valley Water District provides workshops for residents interested in desert landscaping. They are held at the Desert Demonstration Gardens, 3701 West Alta Drive, near the intersection of Alta and Valley View. You will see many plants that will thrive in arid and hot conditions. We cannot emphasize enough how helpful and informative the Desert Demonstration Gardens can be. It's also a nice place just to take a pleasant stroll. Call 258-3205 for information about times and for a calendar of other events at the Gardens.

Very important to serious Las Vegas gardeners is a drip irrigation system, which delivers water directly to the roots of trees and eliminates most of the evaporation associated with sprinklers. See your local nursery or a Home Depot store for materials and advice on drip irrigation systems. Home Depot offers classes on Saturdays for landscaping topics as well as other home improvement projects.

Utilities

Water

Las Vegas Valley Water District
1001 S. Valley View Boulevard
Las Vegas, NV 89153
870-4194

Homeowners and renters are required to pay a $100 deposit or present a letter of reference from their previous water company stating that all water bills were paid when due for one year. When you apply for service, ask the representative if they are sending out water conservation showerhead kits free of charge. The kit contains showerheads and aerators that will reduce water consumption and thus your water bill.

Electric

Nevada Power Company
6226 W. Sahara Avenue
Las Vegas, NV 89102
367-5555

No deposit is required for a homeowner. Renters should have a letter of reference from their previous electric company stating all electric bills were paid when due for one year or pay a small deposit. There is a $15 connection fee.

Gas

Southwest Gas Corporation
4300 W. Tropicana Avenue
Las Vegas, NV 89103
365-1555

No deposit is required for a homeowner, and you must show proof of ownership. There will be a connection fee of approximately $20. Southern Nevada's Senior Weatherization program is a free service designed to help homeowners (including owners of mobile homes) conserve energy and lower utility bills. The senior must be at least fifty-five years old with an annual income of $22,000 or less. The program is available October through May. Volunteer senior energy consultants will visit your home and offer conservation recommendations. Included in the visit is a selection of free weatherization materials installed by the volunteers. Southwest Gas will also provide you with information you need to find a reputable contractor to replace or repair your heating system.

Sewer

Clark County Sanitation
5857 E. Flamingo Road
Las Vegas, NV 89122
458-1180

Sewer service costs approximately $45 quarterly. No deposit is required.

Trash Removal

Silver State Disposal Service
770 E. Sahara Avenue
Las Vegas, NV 89104
735-5151

Trash pickup takes place twice a week at a cost of approximately $33 quarterly. No deposit is required. Recycling is included in trash removal and takes place on its own calendar. Ask Silver State for your free recycling bins.

Telephone

Sprint/Central Telephone
330 S. Valley View Boulevard
Las Vegas, NV 89153
244-7400

Basic telephone service will cost approximately $12 per month, plus a onetime connection fee of approximately $40. Depending on your credit history, there may be a deposit required. Nevada has two area codes. Be careful here. Sprint is very serious about receiving on-time payments and will not wait until the next billing cycle before turning off your service—costing you a $75 reconnect fee. Southern Nevada's code is 702. Rural and northern Nevada's area code is 775. Other local telephone services are listed in the phone book.

5

Job Search

Contrary to popular legend, not everyone in Las Vegas deals blackjack for a living. Although casino employees make up a sizable percentage of the employment picture and are part of a colorful subculture, there are more construction workers than card dealers in southern Nevada.

With 35 million visitors a year, Las Vegas is a service-based, tourism-driven economy with all that that implies. Compared to other regions, jobs are plentiful here but traditionally have not paid as well as work requiring more education and training.

In 2001, a Las Vegas Perspective Study found that 14.4 percent of the 680,000 southern Nevadans who held jobs were employed directly by the gaming and resort industry.

A UNLV study released in 1998 put it this way: "As Las Vegas continues to encourage both commercial and residential development, job growth will continue to be concentrated in these lower paying service industry jobs (gaming and construction). Furthermore, when designing an effective growth strategy, the Las Vegas metropolitan area will need to ensure that it has a well trained labor force for the future."

That Clark County labor force continues to expand at a staggering pace with a 5.5 percent unemployment rate in 2001. In 1995, approximately 437,000 county residents held jobs. By 2001, it was 680,000. The number of working women rose to 357,479 with a median age of 42 years and more than 70 percent noting at least some college experience.

Much of the face of the Las Vegas Valley is aging gracefully. State officials project a continued migration of seniors to the warm climate and friendly tax structure of Southern Nevada. A 1996 study conducted by the Center for Applied Research bears that out. The study showed seniors are moving here for the climate (46 percent), lower taxes (43 percent) and retirement (40 percent).

As the competition for stable employees has increased, the pay scale has improved. Nevada was a national leader in income growth in 1994 and 1995. Through the second quarter of 1996, Nevada remained the country's leader in work creation with

56,000 new jobs in the previous twelve months. Las Vegas, first the previous year, dropped to fifth best in the nation, according to Arizona State's Blue Chip Job Growth Update.

A sample of the mean average hourly wage rates: Casino cage workers, $11.47; receptionists, $10.02; news reporters, $18.95; computer programmers, $25.46; network systems analysts, $23.01; carpenters, $20.17; laborers, $13.46; chefs, $15.06; paralegals, $20.57; auto mechanics, $18.41; janitors, $9.41; landscape workers, $8.85; financial managers, $33.98; hairdressers, $8.80; heavy equipment truck drivers, $16.38; taxi drivers, $12.42.

Nevada also is a right-to-work state, which means employees can be fired at the will of the boss. For no reason, but not for a bad reason. After a multimillion-dollar settlement by Hilton Hotels, the heavily lobbied state legislature severely limited punitive damage awards in cases of wrongful termination.

It is important to generate job leads before moving to Las Vegas. Even in a boomtown, the world is a pretty cold place when you are out of work. The longstanding cliché of the carefree new resident who dashes into a casino and lands a high-paying job as a blackjack dealer is largely the stuff of fiction. In today's Las Vegas, even the card dealers must undergo training and background checks—including drug testing at many resorts—before ever getting near the casino floor.

The best casino jobs at the best resorts are coveted positions that people often work many years to attain. Not only do they pay well, but there is a philosophical shift at many casinos when it comes to employee relations. In the past, the unwritten motto went something like this: "Dummy up and deal." Today, a prospective employee is likely to be required to fill out a job application, as well as undergo an oral and written test. Prior to the opening of the MGM Grand Hotel, prospective employees not only had to complete the paperwork, but they also were asked to sing and dance as if trying out for a chorus line. Old timers scoffed at that, but Grand executives succeeded in finding not only the friendliest workers available, but a few good singers as well.

Here is a Vegas reality for women in the wage-earning end of the gaming industry. If you want to work as a cocktail waitress, you will be forced to wear what, at many resorts, amounts to little more than a bikini, a swatch of fabric, and high heels. Although the jobs pay well when tips are considered, they are not for the faint of heart—or the overweight, middle-aged, or pregnant. The job is one of the bastions of male chauvinism in the casino industry.

In Clark County, approximately 50 percent of workers are employed in service-oriented positions. With so many people in service jobs, it makes sense that there would be fewer working in professional positions. Sure enough, professional people make up only 13 percent of the total workforce, compared to 16.6 percent for the rest of the nation.

The median income per Las Vegas household

in 1994 was $35,895, substantially higher than the national average. Although approximately 40,000 casino employees are represented by the Hotel Employees and Restaurant Employees International Union, better known as the Culinary Union, wages and working conditions vary from one resort to another.

The average hourly wage for a blackjack dealer is approximately $5, but that number is deceiving. Casino employees make a substantial part of their pay from tips. It is not uncommon for blackjack dealers at Strip hotels to receive more than $100 a day in tips. Add to that the $40 daily wage and you have a respectable day's pay.

Here are a few average hourly wages for traditional jobs in the hotel/casino industry: Bartender, $10.77; cashier, $9.03; change person, $7.72; cook, $11.57; food prep, $10.32; front desk clerk, $9.91; housekeeper, $10.28; maid, $8.75; slot mechanic, $13.15; waiter or waitress, $6.86 (tips not included).

All gaming industry workers must obtain a sheriff's card, which has long been one of the "Catch-22s" of the southern Nevada bureaucracy. You need a sheriff's card to work in a casino, but you need a job in a casino before obtaining a sheriff's card. New workers must obtain a referral from their employer before making the trip to 601 East Fremont for the card. The cost is $20 cash, and the card is good for three years. Bring two forms of identification. Also keep in mind that many Nevada employers require preemployment drug testing.

Then there is the Techniques of Alcohol

Management card, or TAM card. In Nevada, all workers who serve, sell, or come in contact with alcohol must obtain a TAM card. Here's how to get one: attend a four-hour class, pass an easy test, and pay a nominal fee. The card is good for five years. The office is located at 557 East Sahara Avenue, Suite 223.

To work as a food handler or in child care, you must obtain a health card. The health district will give you a TB test and a two-hour class. The cost is $10 for the certificate, which you can obtain prior to being hired. The Clark County Health District is located at 625 Shadow Lane.

The Yellow Pages are riddled with employment services, the best of which offer assistance at no cost to the worker. Also the local newspapers have large parts of the classified section devoted to employment opportunities. Some of the jobs are not ideal, but they are a good place to start. The *Las Vegas Review-Journal* publishes several pages of employment opportunities. New hotel-casinos, homes, shopping centers, and industrial complexes are being built every year, so the job outlook remains high. The availability of work is one of the advantages of living in a boomtown.

6

Boomtown Education

Clark County School District

Clark County faces a crisis in K-12 education that cannot be understated. The economic prosperity that has attracted thousands to the desert has overwhelmed the Clark County School District's educational infrastructure. With the growth of the late nineties, Las Vegas became a great place for teachers to find work, but an increasingly harsh place for students to find a quality education. That's not all the fault of the school district administration, headed by Superintendent Carlos Garcia.

The simple fact is, the valley has reached the point where it has barely enough seats for its students. As a result, much of CCSD's budget must be earmarked for construction of new schools. With per-pupil funding below the national average, even simple textbooks are hard to find at some schools. It is clear that all of southern Nevada's economic success has not benefitted its children.

Nevada has the highest teen suicide rate and the second highest teen pregnancy rate in the nation. Its drop-out rate is at the top year after year. (It was 11.7 percent in 1994.) Its teen death rate is fourth highest, and it has the highest teen incarceration rate. While growth and the Las Vegas lifestyle are contributing factors, Nevada's traditional political philosophy also plays a role. The same low tax rates and libertarian bent that attracts so many to the state reveals itself at the bottom line when it comes to paying for the education of children.

In an attempt to resolve the education crisis, community leaders have lobbied hard for the voter passage of multimillion-dollar bond issues to build new elementary, middle, and high schools as fast as they can be constructed. A recent study showed that in percent of income devoted to education, CCSD ranks the lowest in the United States, with the exception of Arizona. Critics of bond issues say they don't want to give money to a school district that spends so inefficiently.

Clark County has the nation's sixth largest school district. There are 266 schools (up from 184 in the mid-1990s) and 244,684 students. There are 33 high schools, 45 middle schools, 166 elementary schools, 16 alternative schools and six special schools. During just the 2001-2002 school year, the CCSD built 16 new schools. The school district headquarters (referred to by locals as the "Ed Shed") is located at 2832 East Flamingo Road. Phone number: 799-5011.

Hundreds of new teachers are hired before the start of each school year, and CCSD now offers a $2,000 signing bonus to new teachers to entice them to come to Nevada rather than another district. It has proven difficult to keep teachers in the fold, however, as statistics show that many new teachers leave the school district within five years.

The powerful Clark County Classroom Teachers Association, also known as the Teachers' Union, has not managed to obtain cost of living raises for its teachers for a number of years, and the union has found its members, unhappy with the representation they are receiving, are leaving the union and going it alone, or joining smaller alternative unions.

Many elementary schools are on a year-round schedule to accommodate the large number of students. The high schools and most middle schools remain on traditional nine-month schedules; but middle schools on year-round schedules have different calendars than year-round elementary schools. It would take some wizardry to plan a vacation around that! Check with the school district for more information on particular schools.

Students must be five years old on or before September 30 to enter kindergarten and six years old on or before September 30 to begin first grade.

To register your child, you must bring a certified birth certificate, up-to-date immunization records, two proofs of address (utility bill and rent receipt, for example), and the name and address of the previous school attended, if any. No proof of citizenship is required. The Clark County Health Department, 625 Shadow Lane, Las Vegas, NV 89127, offers free immunizations.

Parents may choose to have their children apply to one of several so-called "magnet" middle schools and high schools. These schools specialize in various areas of intense study not offered at the standard schools. Magnet schools allow students to choose educational experiences based on their interests. You must apply early and obtain letters of recommendation from previous teachers to be considered. There are very few seats and many qualified students.

The school district's ponderous size and skyrocketing population have led to many challenges in the quality of the education children are experiencing. Test scores show CCSD's students fall just below the national average, and superintendent Garcia is determined to see that change. He has developed a plan called "A+ in Action" designed to increase accountability for student achievement in which all teachers, students and parents take responsibility for student learning.

Seven CCSD schools identified as being "in need of improvement" are being operated not by CCSD but by Edison Schools, the nation's largest private manager of public schools. Six elementary schools and one middle school are affected by this new course of action, and results are not yet in on whether Edison can help improve test scores. One interesting point here is that Edison school students wear uniforms.

For adults needing to complete their high school education, several alternative schools are available, offering classes with flexible hours to fit your work schedule.

The district has a place for everyone, and offers six special schools for students with various challenges. School district personnel will assist you in choosing the best setting for your child with special needs.

Private schools

Private schools in Clark County must be licensed by the Nevada State Department of Education. Many such private schools are affiliated with churches. All are listed in the local telephone directory. One helpful question to ask when considering a private school is whether its faculty is required to be licensed to teach. (Many private schools okay non-licensed teachers.)

Cost is a definite factor in choosing a private school, and is not directly related to the quality of the school. The most affordable private schools are church-related, starting at a few hundred dollars per month. St. Anne's, St. Viator's, St. Francis, St. Elizabeth, the Hebrew Academy and Mountain View Lutheran are some of the parochial elementary schools, and Bishop Gorman and Faith Lutheran are the best-known church high schools.

Cost rises dramatically for the non-parochial private schools. Merryhill Academy (with several locations) offers K-8 with small class sizes and a very good reputation, but many parents report paying over $1,000 per month (more for private lessons such as music). Las Vegas Day School at 3198 South Jones is also a K-8 facility and charges several hundred dollars per month.

The Meadows School, Pre-K through 12, is a 40-acre campus in Summerlin, and has a wonderful reputation academically. Founder Carolyn Goodman boasts a 100% 4-year college placement for its graduates. Again, the price is high, but financial aid is available.

Costs soar at Challenger School, which has campuses in Summerlin and Henderson for preschool through middle school.

Home Schooling

Home schooling is extremely popular in Las Vegas, although it requires a dedicated stay-home parent. The Clark County School District will provide you with a list of "home educator consultants" with whom you must "consult" for a fee if you have not home-schooled before. Through these consultants, you can develop a plan for your student's learning and gather any curriculum materials available. You must file a "Notice of Intent," a 15-page application, a list of educational goals and a 180-day instruction calendar. Your consultant will help you with all these things.

Most parents home-school their children through 8th grade, then transfer them to a regular high school. The reason? In Nevada, your child can only obtain a GED (an equivalency diploma) rather than a high school diploma if home-schooled. If your child begins gathering high-school credits by 9th grade, he or she will have enough time to accumulate the 22 credits necessary to graduate high school. If you wait until 10th grade or later, your child will not graduate (at least on time) because there will be a credit deficiency.

For more information on home schooling, call Home Schools United at 870-9566 or the Association of Home Schooling Families at 631-3607. The Clark County School District home instruction office, directed by Marge Comeau, is 799-8642.

Community College of Southern Nevada

If Las Vegas faces a crisis in elementary education, the Community College of Southern Nevada is progressing nicely. Although crowded, it continues to successfully pursue its mission: to provide affordable, practical course work for adults with short-term and long-range educational goals.

Las Vegas is home to CCSN's dental hygiene program, rated number two in America. The culinary program is ranked third. The community college also has nursing and theater programs, and the variety of courses offered range from sports betting and the basics of electricity to English composition and Nevada history.

Three campuses allow students from each side of town convenient access to classes. The main campus is on East Cheyenne Avenue in North Las Vegas. There is a campus on West Charleston Boulevard, on the west side of town; and the third campus is in Henderson. CCSN offers many programs designed to keep people involved in education. GED preparation courses help students sharpen skills in math, reading, and writing before taking the high school equivalency test. The "first course free" program helps Nevada high school graduates who have never attended college. Also available is the Silver Sage College program for seniors, making CCSN classes free of charge for seniors over sixty-two years old. In addition to traditional financial aid programs, veterans may be eligible for Veterans' Administration education benefits. Students with disabilities can take advantage of special counseling and other services provided by Access to Community College Educational Support Services (ACCESS). The CCSN Planetarium presents wonderful movies in a 360-degree dome. After the last performance, weather permitting, telescope viewing is available.

University of Nevada, Las Vegas

In addition to its high dropout rate, Nevada ranks last among states in sending students to college.

The national average for students attending some college is 53.5 percent. In Nevada, the rate is only 32.8 percent. Governor Kenny Guinn hopes to remedy the situation by using the state's cigarette lawsuit settlement monies to establish the Millennium Scholarship program. Each and every Nevada high school student who maintains a "B" or better average receives a full four-year college tuition scholarship to attend a Nevada college.

Unfortunately, many students receiving the scholarship have not performed well in college; some were so ill-prepared that remedial courses had to be offered them before they could take standard college freshman courses. Initially there was a requirement that Millennium students flunking college courses would be made to repay the scholarship money; then the state legislature stepped in and dropped that rule.

Newcomers to Southern Nevada probably know the University of Nevada, Las Vegas, from its reputation as a college basketball powerhouse. But it's more than that. It also is one of the nation's fastest-growing state universities—and one of the youngest. The growing pains are evident in crowded classrooms and difficult course scheduling. University President Carol Harter appears to be adjusting to the infrastructural stresses, but has had trouble convincing the world of the quality of a UNLV education. *U.S. News & World Report* recently ranked UNLV as a "third tier" university, a low ranking. The good news is that they also reported that UNLV students seem to graduate with a relatively small debt—46% of UNLV students graduate in debt, and the average debt is $11,600. That may seem like a lot, but compared to other universities, it ranks among the lowest number of students in debt and the lowest debt itself.

UNLV offers nearly 140 undergraduate, master's, and doctoral degree programs in eleven colleges. All UNLV programs are accredited by the Northwest Association of Schools and Colleges. The university operates on a semester calendar, with two semesters of approximately sixteen weeks each, plus three short summer sessions between May and August. Application deadlines are July 15 for fall semester and December 15 for spring semester. Students must be fully immunized prior to registering for classes. Contact the Student Health Center for more information at 895-3370. Residence and dining halls are available for students wishing to live on campus. Numerous financial aid programs are also available to students, including grants, loans, scholarships and employment programs. Its 335-acre campus can be seen by guided tour Monday through Friday through the Office of Admissions (call 895-3443 for an appointment).

Vocational Training

Southern Nevada has to be the center of the universe for private schools offering practical training for working adults. Dozens of occupational schools are available for training in specialized fields such as bartending, dog grooming, truck driving, cosmetology, casino dealing, interior design, floral design, and real estate. A warning here: Many students complain of a lack of ability to find suitable employment upon completion of these programs, and they often graduate with thousands of dollars in federal student loans to pay off.

For more information, contact the school or the Commission of Postsecondary Education, 1820 East Sahara Avenue #111. Phone number: 486-7330.

7

This is the City

"Las Vegas is a city in statistics only. In every other respect, it is a jungle—a jungle of green-felt crap tables and slot machines in which the entire population, directly or indirectly, is devoted to fleecing tourists. There were 12 million of these in 1962 (17 million in the state), and the number has been increasing each year. They come to gamble or to have a fling or out of curiosity, and Las Vegas embraces them all, eager to satisfy their craving for gambling—or any vice—with a flourish not seen since Cecil B. De Mille's last Roman spectacle."

Kind of scary, isn't it?

That's the way investigative reporters Ed

Reid and Ovid Demaris sized up Las Vegas in their classic 1963 book, *The Green Felt Jungle.*

One peek at the seamy side of Sin City through the eyes of Reid and Demaris and it's a wonder anyone would want to even visit Las Vegas, much less move there. *The Green Felt Jungle* captured the public's fascination with the prurient nature of the city, but it failed to paint a full picture or depict life outside the so-called jungle. With its history of organized crime activity, and by the very nature of the casino business, Las Vegas has developed a dark reputation that persists to this day.

In part, that reputation is deserved, for any place that generates as many billions in cash revenue as Las Vegas is bound to attract an army of scam artists and cheap hoods. That reputation, much like *The Green Felt Jungle,* fails to tell the whole story of life in southern Nevada.

According to state statistics, for every 100,000 Nevadans, there are 870 adults on probation, 326 on parole, and 460 in prison. In the past decade, Nevada's prison population has increased by more than 100 percent. In a nation that incarcerates more of its citizens than any on the planet, Nevada is first in the country in locking up its convicted felons.

"The reality is, crime is going down," Sheriff Jerry Keller told a group of reporters in May 1996. "This is a very safe city, one of the safest of the major cities.... This may very well be the safest tourist city in the world."

Ah, there it is. Las Vegas is a safe place—for a

tourist city. With billions flowing through the valley, and more than 30 million visitors each year, southern Nevada never will be looked upon as just another American metropolis with one million residents. Not with some of the state's largest security forces wearing the uniforms of the Mirage, Circus Circus, and Hilton rather than those of the Metropolitan Police Department or Nevada Highway Patrol.

Just where does Las Vegas rank compared to other cities?

With approximately 7,300 crimes per 100,000 individuals, in 1995 Las Vegas checked in around 100th among the nation's largest cities, according to FBI and Morgan Quitno Press reports. In the late 1970s, Las Vegas held the dubious distinction of being America's least safe city, but in the past two decades the trend has been more positive. Although the number of crimes committed has risen as the community has grown, the city actually has become statistically safer in many categories. In 1995, there were 60,163 crimes reported from a population of 824,050—not including another 30 million visitors. Rapes and robberies have declined, but the number of homicides—often attributable to the increase in street-gang violence—has continued to rise. The increase in gang-related activity is part of the price southern Nevada is paying for its growth. In 1995, 506 drive-by shootings were investigated by Metropolitan police.

Money magazine recently changed Las Vegas's ranking from 5th to 114th on its list of Most Liveable Cities in the United States during that period, in part because of the troubling lifestyle trends, including air quality and criminal activity. Here again, Nevada's low-tax, libertarian philosophy reveals itself in a distinct lack of police officers per capita (approximately 2 per 1,000 citizens) as compared to other American cities. Although voters pass bond issues almost annually that call for more police officers, the community lags behind in the number of public servants, if not service.

Then there are the quasi-legal business activities that attract attention to the city's eccentric side. Many nude- or partially nude-dancing clubs can be found in Las Vegas. Once they obtain the proper licenses, they are legal businesses that just happen to be hot spots of illegal activity. Prostitution is illegal in Clark County, but you wouldn't know it by reading the Yellow Pages "entertainer" advertisements.

Although legal prostitution takes place in neighboring Nye County, which includes Pahrump, the illegal racket flourishes in Las Vegas. There are also a handful of sex-tease clubs, in which the nude working women inside promise more than they deliver. Tourists are asked to purchase extremely expensive nonalcoholic drinks, presumably to pay for sex. However, after customers spend hundreds of dollars for $3 and $4 bottles of sparkling juice, they are escorted to the door by bouncers who handle complaints their own way. Most customers do not complain to police, since they themselves were attempting to break the law by paying for sex in Clark County. A UNLV study on the subject concluded the following: "The cities of Las Vegas,

North Las Vegas, and Henderson should examine the problems of Florida and not follow in its footsteps. Crime in the Las Vegas valley is on the decline, but is still above the national average. The continued growth of the valley will surely create more instances of crime and place more burdens on the criminal justice system."

* * *

What happened to the Bugsy Siegel types, anyway? Contrary to what some of today's MBA-toting casino operators would have the world believe, organized crime still operates in southern Nevada. According to the FBI, the remnants of the traditional mob can be found in the areas of illegal bookmaking (where they offer credit to players) and high-interest loan shark loans (which often are made to degenerate gamblers and desperate businessmen). But federal law enforcement has placed La Cosa Nostra below violent street gang-related crime and white-collar crime on its priority list. The days of the mob operating openly in a casino's front office are over, but the shadow of organized crime has managed to survive decades after *The Green Felt Jungle* fell from the best-seller list. New residents soon discover that, for all its hype and bluster, when it comes to crime, Las Vegas is a big city like any other.

8

Getting the
Vegas Idea

Imagine working in a whiskey distillery and insisting
on constantly sampling the wares. You would be at
best foolish and at worst an unemployed alcoholic.

It's that way in Las Vegas with gambling. It's no
shame to take a drink, or in this case, to play the
slots or sit at a blackjack table. But it is the worst sort
of folly to think that you can gamble regularly and
expect to pay your monthly mortgage and utilities,
much less put food on the table.

This is not a diatribe against the evils of gambling. Far from it. Las Vegas was built on cards and
dice and the wonders of the house edge. It is safe to

say there would be no boomtown if it weren't for the gold mines that operate disguised as casino resorts.

With that said, you need to remember one thing when you move to Las Vegas: Gambling is for tourists, not locals.

Of course, you might not know that by walking into any of a thousand bars, supermarkets, and convenience stores that have slot machines. And you might think gambling is especially for locals after strolling into one of more than a dozen locals-focused casinos such as the Palace Station and Arizona Charlie's. Locals casinos are filled with movie theaters and restaurants and attract droves of customers. All well and good. They can provide entertainment, but they can also lead to problems for people who aren't in Las Vegas for a hot weekend or fun-filled week.

Locals are different from tourists, and you must never forget that. Fact is, every foolproof system for beating the house has one common denominator: a fool behind it all. It is hard to stress this enough.

The gambling business has put food on countless tables and sent thousands of kids to college. Gambling has ruined countless lives and shattered families like carnival glass. Working in the industry is one thing; pretending you will get rich as a player is another. In fact, many casino executives no longer refer to their business as gambling. Because, they privately note, there is no gamble involved. The house edge is too strong. Instead, they prefer to view gamblers as guests who "rent space" at the slot machines and table games.

Even good gamblers bust out. Even the best sports bettors. Even the world's greatest poker players. Even Nick the Greek. Even Jimmy the Greek. If they all fall short occasionally, what reasonable chance do you have?

The answer is, no chance at all.

With that said, it does not mean that if you play a roll of quarters in a video poker machine that you will become some glassy-eyed, slack-jawed zombie forever chasing Lady Luck's petticoat. Hardly. For many people, gambling is fun and entertaining. A sports bet is a great way to maintain interest in an otherwise boring football game. Dropping a bucket of change into a slot machine passes the time and can be a lot of fun—especially if you take advantage of the inexpensive food and drinks casinos offer their customers.

That really is the lesson of this chapter: If you gamble, go for the value and never lose sight of what you are doing. If you gamble, you will lose. Perhaps not the first time, but eventually. If you gamble a little, you will call it entertainment. If you gamble a lot, you will call it the dumbest thing you ever did. Gambling is for tourists and people with money to burn.

All right. The sermon is over. You have listened, contemplated the facts of life inside the casino, and still you want to try your luck.

No one can blame you. It's pretty exciting hitting a jackpot or turning over a card and making 21. So if you're going to gamble, here are a few tips:

First, never play the big wheel in any casino. It's

a carnival sucker bet that gives the casino a whopping big percentage of your wager. Stay away from Keno, too. It takes 25 percent of your bet. Shy away from gimmicky card games such as Caribbean poker and red dog unless you want to play for the sheer fun of playing and observing your money do strange things before it is drawn into the casino coffers.

Roulette may be fun to watch, but American roulette with its "0" and "00" is a game for lollipops. Don't you be one.

Blackjack is an easy game to understand, but a difficult one to beat. Card counting is supposed to be an easy path to riches, but most card counters die broke. The casino has a dozen ways to frustrate card counters. Still, it won't hurt to read a book on blackjack to learn what card counting is all about.

Craps and baccarat give you the best odds for your money and are not difficult to understand. A good book can teach you either game in a matter of a few minutes.

A savvy book on casino games and the easiest to understand was written by my publisher, Lyle Stuart. Its title is *Winning at Casino Gambling*, and $18 gets you a copy at your local bookshop.

Most important: Never bet more than you can lose.

And remember, gambling is not for working people who plan to live and prosper in the world's largest casino city.

9

Desert Culture

One of the raps on living in Las Vegas is that it is devoid of cultural activity. Ballet companies across America might suffer from a lack of public support and funding, but Las Vegas is bound to be criticized for not being more civilized.

Face it, the city is an easy target. When you promote the world's largest hotels shaped like pyramids, castles, and fantasy lands, and offer topless revues, cheap buffets, and acres of free parking, it's hard to blame people for not appreciating your more polished side.

But the fact is, Las Vegas is growing up. Slowly, to be sure, for its libertarian side is unlikely ever to support taxpayer-funded operas and dance festivals, but it is maturing just the same. Today, more than ninety not-for-profit arts and cultural organizations are registered locally. The mother of all arts groups is the Allied Arts Council, which keeps track of each organization. (Call 731-5419 for information and listings.) It's not the only clearinghouse for the fine arts. There also are arts councils in Henderson (458-8855) and Boulder City (294-5058).

Then come the venues. The Cashman Field Theater offers 1,940 seats; the Government Center Amphitheater downtown has 3,000 seats and is home to popular jazz concerts. The $2 million Sammy Davis Jr. Festival Plaza Amphitheater offers 500 seats and a variety of acts throughout the year ranging from bluegrass and jazz to traditional African and Hawaiian music.

The University of Nevada, Las Vegas on Maryland Parkway offers a year-round schedule of events and is highlighted by the Charles Vanda Masters Series at the 1,885-seat Artemus W. Ham Concert Hall. The Vanda Masters Series, which attracts the greatest names in classical music, has been around since 1976—that's ancient history by Las Vegas standards.

In September, Nevada Shakespeare in the Park performs the Bard's works in Green Valley. The festival draws an average of 25,000 people a year to the outdoor plays at Foxridge Park. And December's presentation of "The Nutracker" by Nevada Dance Theater at the Rio Hotel is a favorite of locals.

There are plenty of places to view local theater and dance, as well as the work of local and regional artists. While Las Vegas is unlikely ever to rival Chicago, New York, or other large cities for traditional culture, it finally is growing into its own.

One of the intriguing aspects of Las Vegas is that most of its best sculptures are not found in museums, but either in public places or in casinos. Most of its wildlife is not located at the diminutive Las Vegas Zoological Park on Rancho Drive, but at the resorts.

You will need a car to discover the culture in southern Nevada.

For statues, Las Vegas must lead all cities in size and age in sheer numbers. In Green Valley, eighteen lifelike sculptures grace the public spaces. Many were commissioned from J. Seward Johnson Jr. and are easily sighted on Green Valley Parkway near Sunset Road. And there is *Circle of Light* by William Limebrook, located in Summerlin. *Flashlight* by Claes Oldenburg graces the campus of UNLV.

No casino offers more sculptures than Caesars Palace, which features marble replicas of David, the Rape of the Sabines, and two dozen more pieces not to be seen outside of the Louvre.

The valley offers more than two dozen non-profit art galleries. A few include the Boulder City Art Gallery, Charleston Heights Arts Center Gallery, Donna Bean Fine Arts Gallery at UNLV, and the Las Vegas Art Museum.

And no local's life in Las Vegas is complete without a trip to the ever-campy Liberace Museum. Any place offering the world's largest rhinestone on display can't be all bad. It also features the world's loudest costumes worn by the late entertainer.

Those preferring more traditional museums will find the Las Vegas Natural History Museum, Nevada State Museum and Historical Society, and the Old Mormon Fort State Historic Park not only quaint but also informative.

The Guggenheim Las Vegas & Guggenheim-Hermitage at the Venetian, 3355 Las Vegas Blvd. South, telephone 414-2440, is resort owner Sheldon Adelson's contribution to the world of fine art in Las Vegas.

The Elvis-a-Rama at 3401 Industrial Road, telephone 309-7200, is heavenly if you love the "King."

The Marjorie Barrick Museum of Natural History at UNLV is free and full of desert animals and Nevada natural history. The Clark County Heritage Museum at Boulder City is home to a "Nevada Home" exhibit as well as railroad cars and the original Boulder City train depot. Don't expect the Smithsonian, but be prepared to gain genuine insight into the colorful heritage of the city and state.

For those who need to get their culture from the airwaves, KNPR (89.5 FM) is the valley's National Public Radio station and offers classical music, news, and commentary. KUNV (91.5 FM) offers jazz all day and alternative rock all night. On the weekends, it features an eclectic schedule ranging from folk and bluegrass programs to shows in Spanish, French and German. KLVX Channel 10 is the public television station and carries the traditional programs.

Libraries

In the early 1990s, and thanks to the passage of an $80 million bond issue, the Las Vegas-Clark County Library District more than doubled. So did the number of private bookstores. With fourteen library branches and thirteen rural libraries, the district has more than 500,000 active library users. The libraries are run by trained staff and approximately 4,500 volunteers.

Following the national trend toward specialization and computerization has been a challenge for southern Nevada library officials. They have been criticized for spending too much on fanciful architecture and computers and not enough on books. But the district continues to respond to the criticism and has spent nearly $5 million in recent years on books.

The libraries in Las Vegas are, for the most part, new and beautiful buildings. Each one has its own specialty and character. All are wheelchair accessible and offer a children's section.

The West Charleston library, in the southwest sector, has the only public medical and health science collection in southern Nevada. It also offers a 289-seat lecture hall.

The Rainbow library, in the northwest, has an outdoor amphitheater with seating for 500 people and a meeting room for 160 people.

The Summerlin library has a beautiful 291-seat theater which allows community and children's groups to perform in a first-class atmosphere. A conference room, study room, and art gallery are also found here. Because it is a large library, it's a good place to find a quiet spot and read.

The Whitney Library in Green Valley has a large Spanish-language collection, 198-seat theater, and a soundproof music practice room.

The largest library, the Clark County Library on East Flamingo Road, has a vast collection of books. It is a good place to go for copies of national and international newspapers.

The West Las Vegas Library has a large 299-seat theater with orchestra pit and dressing rooms.

Perhaps the most interesting library is the Las Vegas Library and Lied Discovery Children's Museum a short distance from downtown. The library offers individual study rooms and the latest in library technology. A word of caution about this library: it is located in an area of town where there is a large homeless population. It's not dangerous, but it can get a bit gamy if you run into library patrons who have not bathed in a few days. Individual study rooms are available, and staff is well-aware of the problem and does everything possible to make patrons comfortable.

The Sahara West Library, in the southwest part of town, is a unique building housing a 150-seat multipurpose room, two small conference rooms, an art gallery, and a microcomputer center.

Not all the books in Las Vegas are sports books and not all the culture comes with its top discarded.

10

Child's Play

Despite intensive marketing to families, Las Vegas remains an adult playground for tourists. Now that you have decided to move to Las Vegas, however, you will begin to see the actual community that often is overshadowed by the megaresorts and out-dazzled by the neon.

One of the perennial misconceptions about southern Nevada is that it is bereft of things to do for young people. Jokes about sending a Las Vegas kid to dealers' school instead of summer camp are as old as vaudeville around these parts. The fact is, although the lifestyle can be hard on families, the community endures and prospers because it continues to evolve into a relatively normal place to raise children—outside the Strip and downtown, that is.

Las Vegas suffers from the usual big-city maladies, and all the stresses that young people face in Boise, Boston and Baton Rouge apply, but those who simply can't find anything for their progeny to do just aren't looking very hard.

It's probably out of habit, but the first place where parents look for their children is inside the tourist corridor. There, they see that nearly every resort offers a high-tech arcade. In addition, Circus Circus has the Grand Slam Canyon Adventure Dome with its double-looping Canyon Blaster roller coaster, and the MGM Grand Hotel and Theme Park has the 250-foot Skycoaster and a faux Hollywood back lot. Atop the Stratosphere Tower, there's the Let it Ride High Roller ride and the truly exciting Big Shot space ride.

But you're probably not tourists anymore, remember? You probably will have to remind yourself of that a time or two.

If you're headed to the Strip, try the Mirage dolphin habitat, where six Atlantic bottlenose dolphins play for the halibut. Or head to Caesars Palace, a resort decidedly not designed with children in mind, and try the Omnimax Theater with its eighty-nine speakers and eighty-nine foot screen with 360-degree viewing. It's not expensive, and some of the movies are educational as well as entertaining. On Rancho Drive, there's the Santa Fe ice rink, one of three rinks in the valley. A window seat at the Santa Fe Buffet provides a grand view of the rink and is an especially entertaining treat during youth hockey or figure skating practice.

In the summer, when the 100-plus-degree temperatures are enough to make you have second thoughts about moving to the middle of the Mojave Desert, the Wet 'n Wild water park on the Strip is a great excuse to cool off. Two tips: Make a day of it by arriving early, and always check the local newspapers for coupons knocking a few bucks off admission for locals.

Municipal pools in town are getting better all the time. Try the Black Mountain pool in Henderson or the YMCA pool in the northwest side of town. These pools, for a very small admission price, offer a huge slide for the big kids, plus a large shallow, sloping entrance to the pool for the little ones. Plenty of grass and shade is provided if you want to bring a picnic.

The Las Vegas municipal pool at Bonanza and Las Vegas Boulevard, the only public pool in the downtown area, is a newly-remodeled and beautiful facility, but not really designed for the enjoyment of the many children who could make good use of it. Its shallow end is five feet, so extreme vigilence is required for those with smaller children.

If one three-minute ride on a roller coaster possibly can be worth taking a forty-five minute drive, then the Desperado at Primm on the Nevada-California border is that coaster. At 225 feet high, it's one of the world's tallest coasters. At a top speed of eighty miles per hour, reaching three Gs in some places, it's not for the squeamish. You won't need the address, but it's located at Buffalo Bill's.

So much for the usual suspects.

Once you've settled in, check out one of the valley's twenty-eight community centers for information on recreation classes, crafts, and workshops. The community centers also have after-school programs available. For instance, the Mirabelli Center offers weight lifting and basketball, and the Lowden Center has a children's library.

For the athlete, nine separate Little Leagues blanket southern Nevada, and for special instruction there's the Las Vegas Baseball Academy run by former professional players Mike Martin and Jerry DeSimone. Clark County offers youth basketball leagues for boys and girls age seven to fourteen. There are two bicycle motocross clubs, four amateur boxing gyms, five swim associations, and more than a dozen public pools, four track and field associations, and numerous youth soccer associations. The Nevada State Youth Soccer Association telephone number is 594-KICK.

There's Pop Warner football and amateur gymnastics, and the City of Las Vegas offers outdoor recreation programs for the physically and mentally challenged.

The fact is, there is plenty to keep young people physically and intellectually active and out of harm's way, but, as in any community, it takes dedicated parents to get the ball rolling.

Now, a quick word about the Southern Nevada Zoological Park on North Rancho Drive. It's small. Tiny, in fact. Approximately fifty animals are encamped on a two-acre site with a small petting zoo and the requisite Bengal tiger, chimp, exotic birds, and reptiles. The zoo's administration has been fined for failing to sufficiently care for some animals, but its problem stems as much from a lack of community support as from a lack of animal husbandry. In a city that touts the wildest animal acts this side of Africa, the lack of support for the community zoo is an abomination.

All great cities have great zoos. Visiting the Southern Nevada Zoological Park is a reminder that Las Vegas is painfully young and still has some growing to do.

11

Active Seniors

The secret is out. Las Vegas has become one of the most popular places in America for people of retirement age. With its friendly tax structure and warm, dry climate, the valley continues to draw thousands of seniors each year.

The face of the Las Vegas Valley is aging gracefully. State officials project a continued migration of seniors to the warm climate and friendly tax structure of Southern Nevada. A recent study conducted by the Center for Applied Research bears that out. The study showed seniors are moving here for climate (46 percent), lower taxes (43 percent) and retirement (40 percent).

Many move into planned communities tailored to their lifestyles such as 2,000-acre Sun City or Sun City McDonald Ranch with homes ranging from $100,000 to more than $300,000. Others prefer to buy a condominium or rent an apartment. No matter. Las Vegas has become senior-friendly.

Senior housing developments typically require that at least one person of at least age fifty-five remains in residence. Other adults may live in the home, but anyone nineteen years or younger must be a visitor.

Here are a few senior housing options: The Villas, 850 homes on the northwest side of town, are adjacent to the Los Prados golf course. Homes are priced up to $250,000. Address: 5150 Las Prados Circle.

Quail Estates West, 200 homes in the center of the valley, is near Sahara Avenue at 2851 South Valley View Boulevard. Prices begin in the low $100,000s.

Promenade at the Meadows, in west Las Vegas near Decatur and Meadows Lane, has homes priced from approximately $150,000 and offers twenty-four-hour security, a clubhouse, and a putting green.

El Paseo, 8078 Kinsella Way, also offers a seniors-only neighborhood with a swimming pool, tennis courts, and a security gate.

Las Vegas also has fourteen retirement apartment communities, many with extra features you would not receive at a regular apartment community, such as housekeepers, meal plans, social activities, shuttle buses, and personal care.

Seniors will want to check in with the local office of the American Association for Retired Persons. The AARP is helpful in getting relocating seniors settled and acquainted with southern Nevada. Another address to remember is 340 North Eleventh Street, location of the Howard Cannon Senior Service Center. In all, southern Nevada offers eighteen senior centers offering field trips, speakers, recreation, and workshops.

UNLV offers classes for seniors sixty-two and over free of charge not including lab fees. Summer classes at UNLV are 50 percent off for seniors. UNLV's Continuing Education program offers fun courses designed for seniors.

Those newcomers who haven't lost their wanderlust will want to contact Geraldine Wulf at Senior Tripsters. Telephone: 387-0007. Senior Tripsters is an active travel club for older persons. The group organizes brief and extended outings exclusively for seniors.

Theresa Mataga, coauthor of the first edition of this book, lends her refreshing perspective on her new home. From her introduction to the first edition: "On October 15, 1995, at the ripe old age of sixty-eight, I decided to put excitement into my life, and I moved to Las Vegas. Life in the middle of the desert has been a unique learning experience. Las Vegas residents are enthusiastically awaiting the completion of more than a dozen new resorts and the expansion of many old favorites. The towns-people brace for the impending boom that will bring job growth and opportunities for advancement. Las Vegas is like a butterfly emerging from a cocoon. By the twenty-first century, Las Vegas will spread its wings in bright and colorful glory.

"Las Vegas is a city in perpetual motion. It is a melting pot of languages, cultures, and religions, yet everyone shares a common bond. Residents depend on tourists to keep the economy strong; tourists depend on the residents to provide them with a memorable vacation. Both are in harmony." The Las Vegas that visitors view from their hotel rooms is not the same place southern Nevada residents see, and that is as it should be. Tourists can take a walk on the Strip or visit the downtown area known as Glitter Gulch without taking the time to think about the hard work and planning it took to provide them with a memorable vacation. All they know is, everything will be ready for them when they arrive in Las Vegas.

"Las Vegas is a land of opportunity for workers and, increasingly, a home-away-from-home for many senior citizens. Seniors like to play video-poker machines, but they also volunteer their time at local hospitals and homeless shelters. You won't find senior ladies sitting at home in their rocking chairs knitting. Southern Nevada is a place for active seniors." From the executive in his million-dollar mansion to the trash man in his humble abode, everyone has a role in making Las Vegas happen. They are the residents of Las Vegas, and they are indispensable. There are times one must wonder what brought the pioneers to the Las Vegas valley more than a century ago and what brings today's travelers to the middle of the desert. The answer can be found in the hearts of the people who live here. They are some of the nicest people you will ever meet.

"After you have unpacked and settled in to your new residence, it will be time to exercise. For really active seniors, there's the Nevada Senior Olympics. With fifteen events and various age brackets, there's something for everyone."

12

The Right Price

When tourists visit Las Vegas, they rarely leave the Strip or downtown. Now that you're a local, you will want to take advantage of a few of the many things to do outside the sweeping casino districts. This list is by no means complete, but it makes for a good place to start. Best of all, at little or no cost, each entry is the right price. Enjoy!

Marjorie Barrick Museum of Natural History: University of Nevada, Las Vegas, 4505 South Maryland Parkway. Telephone: 895-3381. This museum features exhibits of real desert animals, archaeology, anthropology, and history of Nevada and the Southwest. Smithsonian traveling exhibits are also displayed. There is a gift shop and a two-acre garden. Hours: Monday-Friday, 8 AM to 4:45 PM, Saturday, 10 AM to 2 PM.

Boulder City-Hoover Dam Museum: 444 Hotel Plaza, Boulder City. Telephone: 294-1988. Displays historical artifacts related to the construction of Hoover Dam. Watch a free twenty-eight-minute movie entitled, The Construction of Hoover Dam. Gift shop. Hours: daily, 10 AM to 4 PM.

Bruno's Indian and Turquoise Museum: 1306 Nevada Highway, Boulder City. Telephone: 293-4865. The odd but interesting display offers a view of the history of turquoise mining and jewelry making. A trading post and gallery are on site. Hours: daily, 9 AM to 6 PM.

Barbara Greenspun Lecture Series: Located at UNLV's Artemus W. Ham Concert Hall, the lecture series is free and features top names from the national news pages. This series is by ticket only on a first-come-first-served basis. Limited to two tickets per person. Call the university at 895-4352 for a schedule.

Desert Valley Museum: 31 West Mesquite Boulevard, Las Vegas. This museum displays pioneer vintage quilts, wedding dresses, and more. Hours, Monday-Saturday, 8 AM to 5 PM.

Las Vegas Art Museum: 6132 West Charleston Boulevard. The exhibits in the museum's three galleries change monthly. Excellent collection of work from local artists. The museum's store sells art at reasonable prices. Hours: Tuesday-Saturday, 10 AM to 3 PM, Sunday, noon to 3 PM.

Barrick Lecture Series: Located at UNLV's

Artemus W. Ham Concert Hall, this free lecture series is a local favorite and has attracted guests ranging from President Jimmy Carter to Henry Kissinger. Box office telephone: 895-3801. Tickets are available on a first-come-first-served basis, with a limit of two tickets per person.

Bonnie Springs Ranch Petting Zoo: Bonnie Springs Ranch Road, Old Nevada. Telephone: 875-4300. Located near Red Rock Canyon, the petting zoo features usual and unusual farm animals. A restaurant and barbecue area is available. Hours: daily, 10:30 AM to 5 PM.

Las Vegas-Clark County Library District Film Series: Shown at most branches throughout the year. Free admission. Call your local branch. UNLV International Film Series: University of Nevada, Las Vegas. Programmed by Dr. Hart Wegner, director of film studies at UNLV, the series features a compelling list of international art cinema. Hours: 7 PM each Thursday, Room 106 in Classroom Building Complex. Call for mailing list, 895-3547.

Las Vegas Natural History Museum: Fun, fun, fun. This museum, gift shop, and science store offers a hands-on room for kids, animated dinosaurs, marine life (featuring sharks), a diversity of birds, and an international wildlife room. This nonprofit organization is open from 9 AM to 4 PM daily and is located at 900 Las Vegas Boulevard North. Telephone: 384-3466.

Hoover Dam Tour: It's not free, but it's well worth the drive and the price. Take a thirty-five-minute guided tour of the inner workings of the dam. The tour runs daily from 8:30 AM to 5:45 PM all year. Price: adults, $5; seniors, $2.50; children 12 and under, free. And don't forget to visit the Snacketeria, a forty-seat snack bar near the dam.

Ethel M. Chocolate Factory: In nearby Henderson, a free gourmet-chocolate factory tour awaits you. Watch the candy-making process from start to finish through windows while videos guide the tour. Each visitor receives a free Ethel M. chocolate at the end of the tour—but only one! The two-and-a-half-acre cactus garden adjacent to the factory offers a variety of plant life. Hours: daily, 8:30 AM to 7 PM. Drive east on Tropicana, right on Mountain Vista to Sunset Way, left into Green Valley Business Park, then left onto Cactus Garden Drive. Telephone: 458-8864.

Las Vegas Parks & Recreation Summer Melodrama: Come see a free traveling melodrama at city parks, usually in mid-June. Watch for notices in the newspaper, choose a park near you, and be sure to bring a picnic dinner. Great fun for the whole family, and the price is right.

13

Beyond the City Lights

A mule deer steps out from a stand of mahogany, glances your way, then continues browsing. You know you're not in Vegas anymore.

Although the city is likely never to lose its deserved image as a gambling town, inquisitive locals quickly learn that there is more to living in southern Nevada than green felt and neon.

Cynics might argue that Las Vegas is situated in the middle of nowhere, but enterprising residents long ago discovered that it is close to everywhere.

First, some geography. The sprawling mountain

range that forms the western wall of the valley is called the Spring Mountain Range, which stretches for fifty miles. Mount Charleston, at 11,918 feet, is the highest peak in the range and is snow-capped most of the year. On the opposite end of the valley stands Frenchman Mountain, also known as Sunrise Mountain. To the north, the Sheep Mountains. On the south, the Black and McCullough mountains complete the valley.

Mount Charleston

Now, about that mule deer. It is one of dozens of species that thrive in the Spring Mountain range. The wildlife and vegetation are a stark contrast to the desert floor just forty-five minutes away. The Toiyabe National Forest is noted not only for its pines, cedars, and bristlecones, but also for its thirty species of endemic plants. Dozens of hiking trails crisscross the mountains; the stout of heart will be challenged by a trip to Charleston Peak. For those who don't care to stray far from camp, there are many picnic areas and campsites for stays ranging from an afternoon to a month. Sites fill up early, so it is wise to make reservations. Call (702) 515-5400.

In winter, the contrast with the desert is even greater, with plenty of snowfall in the higher elevations. On the Lee Canyon side is a ski resort, Ski Lee, which has been pleasantly surprising downhillers and skiboarders since 1962. The small operation might pale in comparison to the larger resorts in California and Utah, but there is something to be said for fresh powder only forty minutes from Las Vegas.

If your idea of the call of the wild includes a fireplace and table service, then the Mount Charleston Hotel and Mount Charleston Lodge are more your speed. The hotel features a restaurant and lounge, and the lodge is known for its bar and weekend music.

The best-kept secret on Mount Charleston: Of the million-plus people who make the trip from Las Vegas to the mountain each year, perhaps one in 100 bypasses the lodge and hotel to experience the genuine wildlife to be found a few minutes off State Route 157. The hiking trails are seldom crowded.

Red Rock Canyon National Conservation Area

Head west on Charleston Boulevard approximately fifteen miles and you will reach the entrance to a site that rivals anything on the Strip. First-time visitors to Red Rock are awed by the towering sandstone escarpment that juts from the high desert in a mass of orange and red and tan. The 83,100-acre conservation area is highlighted by a thirteen-mile one-wallop that gives automobile sightseers a sample of the beauty and cyclists a genuine thrill. Burros, wild horses, prong-horned antelope, and desert bighorn sheep roam the area, and the sharp-eyed sometimes will catch a glimpse of migrating tarantulas and a wide variety of snakes, including a few of the venomous kind.

Although hiking trails are abundant, travelers often find themselves at Bonnie Springs Ranch for lunch or dinner, and Old Nevada for a taste of Hollywood's version of the Wild West. Bonnie Springs also offers a hotel, free petting zoo, a miniature train ride, and horseback riding.

Spring Mountain Ranch State Park, just up the road, is an ideal place to picnic and is the site of summer concerts and plays. If you continue on, you will encounter Blue Diamond, a small community with a general store and its own occasional newspaper. Blue Diamond originally housed workers from a nearby gypsum mine, but has evolved into a bedroom community for Las Vegas. A bit of Blue Diamond trivia: the town originally was named Cottonwood after nearby Cottonwood Springs, a watering hole for travelers along the Old Spanish Trail.

Pahrump

On the way to Pahrump on State Route 160, at the summit of the Spring Mountains, is the tiny community of Mountain Springs. The Mountain Springs Bar is crowded on weekends and an ideal place to hear bluegrass music in summer.

Pahrump, sixty miles from Las Vegas, is fast becoming another commuter community. A generation ago, alfalfa and cotton farms were its trademarks. Today it has plenty of casinos, restaurants, grocery stores, and even a winery. It also lies in Nye County, where fireworks sales and brothels are legal.

The Pahrump Harvest Festival in September is a kick for country folks and city slickers alike with its rodeo, parade, carnival, and hoedown.

If you own an RV, be sure to visit the RV Park at Terrible's Casino in Pahrump. It offers a small lake, canoe rentals, plenty of grass for the kids to run around, and various other family-oriented rentals and activities. And you don't even have to gamble if you don't want to.

Jean, Goodsprings, Sandy Valley, Primm

Thirty miles west of Las Vegas on Interstate 15 lies Jean, with its two hotel-casinos and one of the state's medium-security prisons. Eight miles west on State Route 161 is Goodsprings, with its turn-of-the-century homesites and Pioneer Saloon. Goodsprings may not look too developed in 2002, but it was southern Nevada's largest city as late as the 1920s.

Six miles farther on 161, you will drop down into Sandy Valley. Like Pahrump, Sandy Valley also is growing rapidly and becoming a popular place for southern Nevadans wishing to live outside the city lights. The town offers two bars, a café, a grocery store, and an entertaining parade and barbecue on the Fourth of July.

On the Nevada-California state line forty-five miles from Las Vegas is one of the area's grand entrepreneurial statements: a town built by one family, the Primms. Primm, Nevada, is named for gambler Ernie Primm, who settled on the border with a humble service station and a few slot machines. Although the place had been inhabited long before Primm arrived, he envisioned a desert oasis, complete with a hotel, casino, and restaurants. His son Gary carries on the family tradition with Whiskey Pete's, the Primadonna, and Buffalo Bill's, which features the breathtaking Desperado roller coaster.

Boulder City, Lake Mead, Hoover Dam

A dozen miles east of Las Vegas, just beyond the valley, lies idyllic Boulder City. The "best town by a dam site" grew along with the construction of nearby Hoover Dam beginning in 1931, and until 1960 Boulder City remained under the control of the Bureau of Reclamation. Visitors quickly will notice a distinct lack of urban sprawl and slot machines there. In fact, gaming is not allowed within the city limits.

Its parks make ideal places to picnic, and the half-century-old Boulder Dam Hotel is one of the area's precious historic sites. Its restaurant serves superior Italian food, and the Arizona Street area is dotted with shops. The Boulder City/Hoover Dam Museum is a favorite with families.

Carved out of Black Canyon forty miles from Las Vegas, Hoover Dam remains one of the great wonders of Great Depression engineering and ingenuity. Hoover Dam's seventeen generators produce one-fourth the energy consumed by the Las Vegas valley. Most of the energy generated by the 726-foot-high, 660-foot-thick dam is used to power parts of Arizona and Southern California.

Hoover Dam cost $160 million to build in the

1930s, and it was completed on time in a little more than four years. The estimated cost to build it today is $4 billion, but even that figure is deceiving. It does not take into account environmental laws and the usual government cost overruns. By way of example, the dam's new parking garage, visitors center, and elevators cost almost as much to construct as the original dam site.

The tour is well worth the long wait in line just for the opportunity to descend into the bowels of one of the nation's working wonders. The forty-four-story elevator ride is a thrill in itself, although claustrophobics might want to avoid it. Someone on your tour is sure to ask how many people were killed in the construction of the dam (ninety-six), and how many of those are entombed in the dam (none). The whole trip lasts 35 minutes and costs $5 for adults, $2.50 for seniors, and is free to children 12 and under.

Hoover Dam holds back Lake Mead, one of the largest man-made lakes in the world. Its 822-mile shoreline is dotted with nine marinas, which offer a variety of services. The lake is popular with boaters, campers, and anglers, who work the waters for striped and largemouth bass.

The massive Lake Mead National Recreation Area is composed of Lake Mead, Lake Mohave and the surrounding desert from Davis Dam to the south, Grand Canyon National Park to the east, and north to Overton. Nearly 90 percent of the recreation area is desert.

Although you'll find most of the sunbathers

stretched out at Boulder Beach, the Alan Bible Visitors Center offers plenty of information on the lake and area's desert flora and fauna.

Recreation area fees are $5 per car per week or $15 for an annual pass.

A word of caution: The summer heat can be excruciating, running a full ten to fifteen degrees hotter than Las Vegas. Thunderstorms are known to cause flash floods inside the recreation area, so plan ahead.

The lake has nine developed areas, including picnic sites, marinas, camping, and swimming spots. You will also find dinner cruises available on Lake Mead for reasonable rates.

Valley of Fire, Moapa Valley

Nevada's oldest state park remains one of its most breathtaking. Valley of Fire State Park was dedicated in 1935—practically prehistoric on the Las Vegas time line—and for generations visitors have marveled at its red sandstone rock formations and ancient Indian petroglyphs. The park offers campgrounds and a visitors' center.

Newcomers to the Valley of Fire will want to plan to be there during a full moon, when the night lighting sets the sandstone ablaze.

The Moapa Valley, which includes Moapa, Glendale, Overton, Logandale, Meadow Valley, the Moapa Indian Reservation, and Warm Springs, begins approximately fifty miles northeast of Las Vegas. The Clark County Fair in April highlights the year for Logandale.

Just south of Overton is the Lost City Museum, which houses a fascinating collection of Anasazi and Pueblo Indian artifacts. The Pueblos have inhabited the area for centuries, but newcomers are welcome at the museum, which is open from 8:30 AM to 4:30 PM with $1 admission.

Death Valley

If you have a trustworthy vehicle, Death Valley National Park is a fun day-long excursion. The length of the park is 140 miles, with many attractions along the way. One such place is Furnace Creek Visitors' Center, where you can find maps and brochures describing Death Valley; also nature exhibits and slide shows and restrooms are available here.

Badwater is the lowest point in the United States at 280 feet below sea level. The Harmony Borax Works is an interesting trail that leads to an abandoned borax mine.

Death Valley Junction, population seven, is the location of the Amargosa Opera House, where Marta Becket performs a one-woman dance show about ninety-five times per year.

Scotty's Castle, formerly known as the Death Valley Ranch, is a 25-room mansion admired for its fine craftsmanship. It was built near a stream, which provided its occupants with water and power. Daily tours are conducted every hour.

For a good time at Death Valley Junction, visit

the Crow Bar, an old-time bar with few patrons. Sit at the bar and talk to people from all around the world.

Also available up the road from Death Valley Junction is Tecopa Hot Springs, a popular spot for senior citizens. Visit the public bathing houses (separated by sex). No swimsuits allowed, so bring your sense of humor.

Laughlin

This boomtown is like a small Las Vegas. One hundred twenty miles south of town on State Route 163, Laughlin offers more than 8,500 hotel rooms at very inexpensive rates during the week (as low as $19). Las Vegans consider it a dressed-down alternative to the glitzier hotel-casinos in Las Vegas. Until recently it boasted just one movie theater, but many of the hotels offer first-rate concerts. Laughlin sits on the Colorado River; some hotels offer riverboat rides.

No matter which end of the valley you choose, southern Nevada offers much more than the Strip and downtown. Consider this merely a prologue to your own adventures beyond the city lights.

14

Quickie Marriages and Abiding Faith

Many visitors find it odd that religious worship takes place in Las Vegas, a place that gives off such secular vibes, but that's one of the city's many ironies.

Another long-perpetuated myth about Las Vegas is that it has more churches per capita than any other city in America. The remark has found its way into print in dozens of newspapers and many books, and it made for a great comeback when moralists were busy beating up Las Vegas and calling it Sin City and the Devil's Playground, but it's just not the case.

Las Vegas does, however, lead the planet in places to get married. The highest wedding chapels are located at the 1,149-foot Stratosphere Tower on Las Vegas Boulevard. The most famous chapel in the city is the Little Chapel of the West near the Hacienda, and perhaps the funkiest chapel in the city is the Graceland Wedding Chapel, which features an Elvis theme and offers a minister who vaguely resembles the Man from Memphis.

Another misconception is the idea that the Mormon faith makes up a large percentage of churchgoers in the valley. That, too, is false. Although the Mormons might make a strong argument for their devotion to their church, their numbers make up just 6 percent of the Las Vegas population. What they lack in numbers, however, they more than make up for in places to worship. In fact, there are more Mormon churches, 164 in 1994, than any other religious faith in southern Nevada. In fact, there are more Mormon churches than there are Catholic, Methodist, Jewish, and Lutheran places of worship combined. The church also features by far the most recognizable edifice in the form of the Mormon Temple at the base of Frenchman Mountain at the east end of the valley.

Here are the numbers: Catholic, 28 percent; Protestant, 27 percent; No Affiliation, 22 percent; Other, 13 percent; Mormon, 6 percent; Jewish, 5 percent.

Religious organizations are also numerous, such as the Salvation Army, Catholic Daughters of the Americas, Jewish Federation of Las Vegas, St. Jude's Women's Auxiliary, etc. Also there are twenty-five stores that could be called religious book stores. Two radio stations offer religious broadcasting: KILA (90.5 FM) and KKVU (1060 AM).

New residents who settle on the outer edges of the valley may have difficulty finding a specific house of worship close to them. In this boomtown, Sunday morning commutes to church are common occurrences.

If you didn't have faith, you probably wouldn't have had the courage to move to a boomtown.

15

Shopper's Paradise

Las Vegas is a shopper's paradise, but it wasn't always that way. Only a few years ago, the city's population—despite the millions of tourists who visited each year—did not warrant serious attention from the upscale department stores that proliferate larger cities. There were plenty of Sears and JCPenney stores in the local malls and an assortment of specialty shops at the resorts offering furs and custom Italian leather goods, but the finer shops were hard to find.

All that changed as southern Nevada approached the million population mark. It also helped that, in some cases, managers of many major chains began to market toward tourists as well as locals.

The result has been an increase in shopping outlets that are good and getting better. They might even make you feel as if you've never left home. Unfortunately, despite the tremendous growth in population toward the west end of the valley, southwest and northwest Las Vegas are without major shopping malls.

The valley's leading malls:

The Boulevard Mall

This is Las Vegas's largest (and oldest) mall. Shops include Sears, JCPenney, Dillards, Victoria's Secret, and Hot Dog on a Stick. This is a wonderful mall for strolling and people-watching, as well as shopping. 3768 South Maryland Parkway. Hours: Monday to Friday, 10 AM to 9 PM; Saturday, 10 AM to 7 PM; Sunday, 11 AM to 6 PM.

Fashion Show Mall

Located on the Strip at Spring Mountain and Twain, the Fashion Show Mall has more than 100 specialty stores, including the Disney Store, Banana Republic, Sharper Image, and Louis Vuitton. This mall proudly houses the star of all Las Vegas stores, shopper-friendly Nordstrom. This is an upscale shopper's paradise—fun to stroll around, but unless you are wealthy, you will do more window-shopping than buying. Hours: Monday to Friday, 10 AM to 9 PM; Saturday, 10 AM to 7 PM; and Sunday, noon to 6 PM. Telephone: 369-8382.

Forum Shops at Caesars

More than seventy shops and restaurants featuring Guess?, Gucci, the Museum Company, Spago, Planet Hollywood, the Palm Restaurant and the popular FAO Schwartz toy store (two-story horse included). This is a must-see attraction, if only for the ceiling. This is also a super-upscale mall, so bring lots of money or just stroll around. Location: 3500 Las Vegas Boulevard South. Telephone: 893-4800.

Meadows Mall

This mall has easy access to I-15 (take the Valley View exit). Stores include Macy's, JCPenney, Sears, and more than 140 good shops and restaurants. This mall is a nice neighborhood mall and has shops whose prices are within reality. Hours: Monday to Friday, 10 AM to 9 PM; and weekends, 10 AM to 6 PM.

Galleria Mall

The city's newest mall, the Galleria is located in Green Valley, on Stephanie Street between Sunset Road and Warm Springs Road. Shops include Mervyn's California, Baby Gap, Dillards, and JCPenney. An excellent food court. Take I-95 south to Sunset exit.

Belz Factory Outlet World Mall

Includes Bass, Geoffrey Beene, Levi's, Oshkosh, Ruff Hewn, Corning-Revere, Nike. The latest expansion to this mall almost doubled its size. A very nice mall to look for decent deals on top-name items.

Swap Meets

There is one outdoor swap meet, the Broadacres, at the corner of Las Vegas Boulevard North and Lamb in North Las Vegas. This twenty-six-acre shopping area is open Friday, Saturday, and Sunday, with admission 50 cents on Friday and 75 cents on weekends. You will find both new and used merchandise, but arrive early for the best deals. Opens at 6:30 AM

There are a few indoor swap meets, selling all new merchandise. The more popular include the Fantastic Indoor Swap Meet, on the west side of town at 1717 South Decatur Boulevard, and the Boulder-Sahara Indoor Swap Meet, 3455 Boulder Highway on the east side of town.

For antiques and crafts, your best bet is to head to Charleston between Maryland Parkway and Eastern. Here is the center of the antique universe in Las Vegas. A few stores stand out as especially fun or interesting places to shop:

The Red Rooster is a great place, but only go if you have at least two hours to spare. This 25,000-square-foot consignment store offers antiques, unique gifts, and handmade crafts of all kinds. Location: 1109 Western Avenue. Can be difficult to find for newcomers unacquainted with the winding back streets near Charleston Boulevard and Martin Luther King Drive. Go east on Charleston, right on Martin Luther King, left on Wall Street, left on

Western. Hours: Monday to Saturday, 10 AM to 6 PM; Sunday, noon to 5 PM.

The Charleston Outlet offers used clothing and some housewares at extremely low prices. Shop here often because merchandise turns over quickly, and you're likely to find a name-brand treasure in your size. Location: 1548 E. Charleston Boulevard, near 13th Street. Hours: Monday to Saturday, 10 AM to 6 PM.

Garage Sales can turn into quite a hobby in Las Vegas and can be a great way to spend a morning. Check the papers starting Thursday since Friday sales are becoming commonplace. Check again on Friday and even on Saturday early if you want to be thorough and not miss anything. It helps to circle those sales you think will have things you want. Then plan a route and go to each of those sales. But of course you will see signs along the way, taking you off your intended route and into unknown but hopefully fruitful territory.

Garage sale ads in the *Review-Journal* are separated by geographic area, and Las Vegas is divided into four: southwest, northwest, southeast, and northeast. We have found that it's sometimes fun to head to some other part of town and go "garage saling" (yes, a verb) for a change of pace. Boulder City, for instance, is a great little town to visit, but if you can throw in some garage sales, all the better.

The major discount stores are represented in Las Vegas, including Wal-Mart, K-Mart and Target. Business is booming, and you will find more than one of each of these stores on your side of town.

Membership stores such as Costco and Sam's Club offer consumers something different: a chance to pay for the opportunity to shop. For around $35, you can get a one-year membership at each of these stores. Many consumers like the merchandise and the prices and feel the membership fee pays for itself. These stores work better for large families since many of the food items come packed in jumbo sizes. More often, consumers use these stores when planning for parties—and it is nice to be able to buy, say, 25 pounds of ready-to-eat broccoli in one bag when you need it! Both stores have impressive bakeries and delicious cakes for a fraction of the price you would pay at a regular grocery store. One warning: With such an interesting variety of items, you are likely to purchase items you had no intention of buying, and it is an often repeated complaint that you cannot leave these stores without buying more than $100 worth of stuff, even if you had no intention of doing so!

Strip malls in town are unique and take time to get to know. Those closest to your new home will be the first you explore, so begin now! One outstanding strip mall is near the corner of Charleston and Durango and features Pottery Barn and Gap. A couple nicer strip malls are near the corner of Lake Mead Boulevard and Rainbow, featuring Border's Books and Barnes & Noble books, Old Navy, Michael's craft store, two office supply stores, and a dozen or so family restaurants. Look around your neighborhood and you're sure to find something you like.

16

State of the Game

There are no sure things, not even on the fabulous Las Vegas Strip. That was the painful lesson taught in the wake of the terrorist attack on the United States, which resulted in an economic tsunami throughout the casino and tourism industries.

After a decade of record growth, insanely profitable bottom lines, and unprecedented expansion of legalized gambling outside Nevada, the reality of the new world disorder set in. Casino employees were laid off in droves; nearly 30,000 people lost jobs or had their hours dramatically reduced.

"According to our survey of 17 leading gaming companies, 2001 was a disappointing year for gam-

ing operators after two consecutive years of mean-
ingful increases in industry profitability," notes the
January 2002 *McDonald Equity Research Report,* com-
piled by financial analysts Dennis I. Forst and
Jonathan Waite. "...The combination of a slowing
economy, huge interest expenses from industry
consolidation and the impact of the September
11th terrorist attacks caused 2001 gaming industry
pretax profits to return to 1995 levels of about $1.47
billion." Revenues for companies surveyed rose
approximately 1 percent to $24.9 billion before
taxes, depreciation, and other expenses.

Although analysts looked for slight improvements in the corporate performance of the gaming
industry overall in 2002, few were willing to predict
a return to the eye-popping growth of the previous
decade.

Various factors came into play. To name a few:
the impact of competition from Native American
casinos, especially in California; the potential
expansion of Internet gambling; possible tax
increases not only in Nevada but in other states
where Nevada-based companies did business; the
threat of retrenchment of casino expansion in
regions where the business remained controversial;
a possible ban on college sports betting, and the
licensure of major Las Vegas casino developers
Sheldon Adelson, of the Venetian, and Steve Wynn,
formerly of Mirage Resorts, on the Asian island
gambling empire of Macau.

Wynn's Le Reve ("The Dream") resort project
on the site of the venerable Desert Inn illustrated

one of the challenges of Las Vegas after the boom. In part through his own tumultuous business life, in part from the aftermath of September 11, Wynn was said by gaming industry experts to be having difficulty finding suitable financing for his nearly $2 billion project. Although he would take on a partner in the form of a Japanese slot machine manufacturer and pursue big-money contacts in the Far East, Le Reve remained on the drawing board. It was good for Wynn's competitors, who had found in him a spare-no-expense operator capable of drawing legions of customers from other resorts with his polished resorts and catchy themes.

By early 2002, resorts on the Strip and along Southern Nevada's newer gambling corridors appeared to have nearly fully recovered from the economic shock of September 11. Others, however, weren't as lucky.

The biggest loser in Las Vegas was the $1 billion Aladdin, which appeared to be cursed from its 2000 opening. Park Place Entertainment spotted its obviously weak financial and management structure and purchased 30 percent of the 2,567-room resort on its 35-acres site. Its poorly designed entrance and inability to attract customers from a variety of markets appeared to doom it to bankruptcy, which it entered in late September 2001. By February 2002, it sought to liquidate assets. All of which meant that its majority owner, Sommer Family Trust, figured to be roasted when the property was finally sold off for a fraction of its construction price. The fate of its 3,000 employees was uncertain, but it was unlikely that the property would actually close despite its eventual change of ownership. Whether downtown, at the heart of the Strip, or at one of a growing number of neighborhood casinos, the question was not whether the financially troubled gambling halls would shut down, but just who would be the next entrepreneur to come in and take a shot at the potential high returns associated with a successful gaming operation. For companies looking to increase their bottom line, casinos were all but irresistible.

Not all casino operators sacked employees and put a halt to expansion plans. At a time when local casino executives were laying off legions and offering pessimistic forecasts for the economic future of Las Vegas, consider Michael Gaughan a green-felt optimist. Gaughan, chairman of Coast Resorts, which owns the Barbary Coast casino and locals-focused Gold Coast, Orleans, and Suncoast casinos, is proud that he's managed to operate properties for more than 30 years without a layoff. There were hiring freezes and reduced shifts, but he avoided painful layoffs such as those at the Strip megaresorts.

Reliable estimates place the number of workers out of jobs at between 12,000 and 15,000, with employees of industry giants Mandalay Resort Group and MGM Mirage being the hardest hit in the wake of the Sept. 11 terrorist attacks that killed thousands and paralyzed commercial air travel for several days.

Some would call Gaughan's mostly locals operations an apples-and-oranges comparison next to the megaresorts. Approximately 90 percent of Suncoast customers are local. The estimates run 70 percent local at the Gold Coast and 60 percent local at the Orleans. The Barbary Coast, however, draws mostly tourists and has been hurt by the economic downturn in the wake of the terrorist attacks. Gaughan said there were no layoffs there, either. While Gaughan's creative use of scheduling would be sure to raise the blood pressure of labor organizations, and his status as a private operator arguably helped him to act more quickly than the heads of publicly traded companies, it helped enable him to survive without cutting jobs. "I've never had a layoff in my history," Gaughan says. Some of his employees are having their hours cut. The extra boards, used for part-time employees, were frozen, and the company wasn't hiring. While others were preaching gloom, Gaughan says he's roaring ahead with $200 million in expansion plans at the four properties, including a $100 million ice arena big enough to house a minor-league hockey team. He continued plans to build another casino on the far south end of the Strip.

In the new century, Gaughan was one of the last of the Las Vegas iconoclasts. His personal style was rare, but his family, led by patriarch Jackie Gaughan, had made it work for 50 years in Southern Nevada. He displayed something increasingly rare in the new Las Vegas: an understanding of the wage earners who toiled for him. "It's hard to find good employees," Michael Gaughan said. "The ones that are getting hit hardest are the maids, but do you know how hard it is to find good maids? I've got good maids, and I'm keeping them. It looks like I'm going to be all right."

In tough times, a little green-felt optimism goes a long way—and pays dividends. By early 2002, Coast Resorts not only was rolling on its expansion projects but reported business was back to normal.

* * *

While the number of major casino projects planned for Southern Nevada slowed considerably in 2002, the Strip increasingly took on a Miami Beach look with several high-rise, high-end condominium projects underway. Most sparkling was the Park Towers, developed by Irwin Molasky with help from Steve Wynn and sporting an average price of nearly $1 million per apartment. Others, such as the Soffer family's Turnberry Place near the north end of the Strip, was slightly down scale but immensely popular with three towers in various phases of development and prices starting in the $500,000 range. In February, yet another large-scale time-share condominium project was announced for the Strip. Polo Towers owner Stephen Cloobeck unveiled plans for a 30-story, 850-unit development that would cost $240 million and was scheduled to begin in 2004. He called it The Chateau. "We're in the epicenter of what's happening in Las Vegas, and I think The Chateau has the best location, by far, of any time-share project on the Strip," Cloobeck boasted to the *Review-Journal.* In addition to Polo Towers, his Diamond Resorts International owns the 250-unit Jockey Club on the Strip.

* * *

One challenge facing the casino industry in the increasingly scrutinized world after September 11 is the perception in the law enforcement community that its marketing men and women commonly cater to high-rolling criminals.

An article in *The Washington Post* shed light on the questionable love affair between Asian mob figures and corrupt politicians and the casinos of Las Vegas, but in truth cash players of questionable origins have been a sizable part of the industry's marketing for generations. Whether flying in from across the globe or driving in from Los Angeles, the bad guys have often been good players.

One example was the wide-open welcome drug trafficker John Ward received from the Strip casino crowd. The bad guy was a good customer in Las Vegas. You might be surprised just how good. The 31-year-old Ward was sentenced to life in prison without the possibility of parole in 2002 in an Orange County, California, federal court, ostensibly for running a methamphetamine and cocaine trafficking operation that generated more than $1 million a week. One leg of his operation extended from Southern California to Hawaii, where he was suspected of supplying the synthetic super speed "ice" to the islands. According to the *Orange County Register*, Ward ran his meth ring like a corporation. Like Enron, perhaps, for the swaggering dope dealer wasn't shy about showing off his wealth. There were the foreign sports cars worth hundreds of thousands. But a player with a Mercedes, Porsche and Ferrari feels underdressed without a $25,000

Rolex and enough green to buy big diamonds for the femme du jour. Ward had all that and more.

Then there's the cash. Sacks and satchels and suitcases of it, much of it in small bills. He spread it around to friends and associates, and was assisted in his underground corporation by an eclectic crew ranging from regional Hells Angels president Rusty Coones to former Orange County District Attorney Bryan Kazarian. Ward's own parents shared in the crime and profits. Kazarian leaked intimate details of the government's case to his friend the meth-maker. Ward's high-rolling success story was complicated by the numbers.

From 1997 to 1999, Ward gambled away $2.1 million, much of it in the form of small bills, at the Rio, Mirage, Treasure Island, Bellagio, Hilton, Hard Rock, and Mandalay Bay. He was not only a pre-ferred customer who received full complimentary resort privileges, but was a darned efficient loser as well. Surely those casinos must have appreciated that. According to court documents, on March 30, 1998, at the Rio, Ward managed to lose $420,000 in one hour, 25 minutes. The following month at the Mirage, he parted with $220,000 in a little more than three hours. Later that summer at the Mirage, he lost $205,500 in 95 minutes. For a man who loved money so much he was willing to risk a life prison sentence, he sure wasn't shy about handing it across the gaming tables. And all the time he was toting cash around by the sackload, no casino expert suspected he was a less-than-upstanding businessman. At least, not officially.

Although court-authorized wiretaps revealed suspicious dealings between Ward and one casino marketing executive, no one in the casino business was arrested. Sources close to Ward laugh about their former pal's personal lifestyle, which they described as a pimp/gangster hybrid that included gaudy pinstripe suits and gold-heavy jewelry. He was on stage in neon until the day they came to take him away.

Ward's case, while hardly unique, illustrates a tradition that has infuriated law enforcement and fascinated legalized gaming's critics for decades: The bad guys are often good customers.

The law officially requires casinos to insist customers fill out cash transaction reports, and cash players commonly are tracked with their greenbacks segregated. Such window dressing saves casinos from legal entanglements, but it doesn't change the fact they live in a world ruled by plausible deniability.

With keener competition than ever, and an uncertain world market, so-called "recession-proof" Las Vegas finally appeared vulnerable to the same economic forces that effected the rest of the country. The Southern Nevada gaming economy remains powerful and vibrant at many levels, but with casinos proliferating the American landscape, Las Vegas no longer seems quite so invincible.

17

The Real Hughes Legacy

Mention the name Howard Hughes, and a few images pop to mind. First, there's the picture of an eccentric billionaire playboy and aviation mogul who secretly moved to Las Vegas in the late 1960s and began buying up casinos. Then there's the Hughes of even stranger legend, the one whose personal quirks and demons captured the world's imagination for many years.

But what if someone told you that Hughes's legacy wasn't in the hotels he bought, but in the vast sections of raw real estate located outside the Las Vegas he knew that were purchased for a relative pittance?

The less mysterious truth about Hughes is that he was at best a casino landlord whose genius, such as it was, manifested itself in those big land buys.

Today, the Hughes legacy is to be found at the Summerlin planned community developments which line the edge of the valley at the foot of the Spring Mountain Range. In Summerlin, and enormous developments such as American Nevada Corp's Green Valley in Henderson, newcomers will find the "New Las Vegas."

Although some urban planning experts criticize the proliferation of gated communities with their high block walls and lengthy list of conditions and restrictions, these neighborhoods in many ways represent the first real attempt to plan and mold the incredible growth that continues to take place in the valley.

In places like Summerlin, so-called leapfrog zoning has given way to sensible planning, shopping centers that tend to complement neighborhoods, a control of neighborhood bars, convenience stores, gas stations and casinos.

Although the growth of neighborhood casinos throughout Southern Nevada continues to be controversial—local power brokers somehow manage to circumvent the spirit of several restrictions put in place to keep the locals-marketed gambling halls at bay—Summerlin and other similarly minded communities are shaping the future of residential life in the valley. Although the rest of the valley is catching up, these communities were leaders in planning for parks, schools, and fire stations.

Home prices range from slightly more than $100,000 to custom lots and houses worth more than $1 million. In 2001, Summerlin sold 2,976 homes, by its count over 30 percent more than the nation's next biggest master-planned development, The Villages in Orlando, Florida.

As of 2002, more than 20,000 homes had been sold at Summerlin. For upscale buyers, Summerlin's Promontory at The Ridges offers up to three-quarter-acre lots ranging from $350,000 to $950,000. The Ridges also features "Bear's Best Las Vegas," a championship golf course developed by Jack Nicklaus.

Whether they live in Green Valley or Summerlin, residents are increasingly able to take advantage of the completion of the I-215 "beltway" project that continues to complete its ring around the valley. The beltway enables residents of the distant planned developments to reach the heart of downtown and the Strip quickly, or to bypass the center of the urban corridor entirely. In a community known nationally for its traffic problems, the beltway is providing a modicum of relief.

On the retail side, Summerlin continues to expand. (Summerlin is developed by the Howard Hughes Corporation, an affiliate of the Rouse Company, which is known nationally for its mall and other retail development.) More than 3 million square feet of retail space is being developed with Rouse ready to build a 1.5 million-square-foot mall.

One develoment is the 600,000-square-foot shopping center called Canyon Pointe. Located on West Charleston and Pavilion Center Drive, it sits on 62 acres.

All that doesn't include the more than 6 million square-feet of office space set for development at Summerlin over the next 15 years.

Green Valley in Henderson, an 8,400-acre master-planned development that was the vision of the late *Las Vegas Sun* Publisher Hank Greenspun, is now home to more than 60,000 people. Although its 1,310-acre Green Valley Ranch project is now sold out, Seven Hills continues to sell well. Seven Hills is located at the foot of Black Mountain. Home prices range from the $140,000s to more than $200,000 for a single lot. Of course, not all planned communities go according to plan.

The Mountain Spa luxury home development near Floyd Lamb State Park (which locals still commonly call Tule Springs) has only slowly grown on its 637-acre site. After more than 10 years, project developer Jack Sommer, also a part-owner of the bankrupt Aladdin hotel and casino on the Strip, in early 2002 seemed unsure of his future marketing strategy for the upscale residential development. He temporarily ceased selling home lots. At one point, Ritz-Carlton indicated its interest in creating a five-star resort and casino at Mountain Spa. But when its plans changed, so did Sommer's. Model Homes at Mountain Spa sell for from $500,000 to $1.5 million, according to the company.

Summerlin and Green Valley have done nothing less than change the face of the Las Vegas Valley and spread residential and commercial development from the urban center to the far reaches of the foothills.

18

The Yucca Mountain Question

You're moving to Las Vegas, but not long after unpacking your boxes and enrolling your children in school you're sure to be asked a question: What's your opinion of Yucca Mountain?

The Yucca Mountain Project is a plan by the Department of Energy and the nation's nuclear power industry to store approximately 77,000 tons of the country's spent plutonium fuel rods and other radioactive refuse in a repository set 90 miles north of Las Vegas in a place on the edge of the Nevada Test Site called Yucca Mountain.

The project is controversial for many reasons, not the least of which are the health and safety fears of Nevadans who oppose the dump. Public opinion polls taken in late 2001 suggest that as many as 80 percent of Nevadans oppose the dump, but more than 60 percent say they believe it will come to the state despite their protests (in as early as 2010, according to the DOE).

How much should you fear Yucca Mountain? Not as much as some in Nevada's press and political circles might have you believe. But what should be extremely discomforting is the way the project was shoved down the collective throats of all Nevadans.

Although Nevada's nuclear history began in Cold War era with above-ground atomic bomb blasts at the Nevada Test Site (the front gates of which are located 60 miles north of Las Vegas), the Yucca Mountain dump is perceived by the public—and has been spun by the state's political elite—as a very different animal. While the test site was created not only to test our nuclear capability, but as a kind of muscle-flexing deterrent to Soviet aggression, Yucca Mountain is a sop to the nuclear power industry, whose power plants have been safely storing spent fuel rods for many decades but nearly 30 years ago began pushing for a single storage site in the name of safety and political positioning.

After the Three Mile Island incident, the bubble burst on the wonders of nuclear power, and on-site plutonium in highly populated states became a political liability. So, an alternative, permanent site had to be chosen. Nevada was selected in 1987 prior to conducting comprehensive testing at Yucca Mountain for things like earthquake faults (the area has them), groundwater instability (there are signs of that), and dozens of other factors.

Backed by pronuclear Louisiana Senator J. Bennett Johnston, the so-called "Screw Nevada Bill" was passed under protest from this state's diminutive Congressional delegation.

But more than $8 billion and nearly two decades later, the fight is still on with Nevada being dragged ever closer to being forced against its people's will to accept the repository. In the end, government estimates place the cost of Yucca at more than $20 billion.

Although President George W. Bush signed off on the project, Nevada Governor Kenny Guinn vetoed the recommendation, as is his right under law, and Congress was expected to override that veto with simple majority votes in the House of Representatives and Senate, the battle over Yucca Mountain is far from finished. Multiple lawsuits have been filed at the local and state levels against the project, and that litigation could drag on for many years. Although some legal observers point to Article 6 of the U.S. Constitution (which states the federal government has the supreme voice in matters of national interest) as a sign that Nevada eventually will lose its fight, others believe that a lengthy delay in the process could eventually turn the tide. Technological advancements in the treatment and reprocessing of nuclear waste could render Yucca Mountain obsolete in a decade, some scientists believe. Others say the key to stopping the project might lie in alerting other states—the nuclear waste will be transported through as many as 42 states before it arrives in Nevada—to the danger of moving spent fuel through their backyards. As of early 2002, Utah had decided to stand up with Nevada in its opposition to the Yucca Mountain repository.

There are many reasons to oppose the project, but one of the most basic and compelling is the fact there will be few jobs created by the repository. Nuclear industry lobbyists admit that as few as 200 full-time jobs will be filled if Yucca goes on line. Although hundreds of union truck drivers will be employed in moving the miserable muck, with its 10,000-year half-life, Nevada residents won't receive many jobs or economic windfalls from the repository.

What's equally important for new Southern Nevadans is that they understand that Yucca is a political mountain as well as a barren, physical hill located not far from the middle of nowhere.

The actions of Department of Energy Secretary Spencer Abraham, who'd let it be known immediately after taking office that he favored the Yucca Mountain site and who maintained at best a thinly veiled sense of "objectivity" about the project, serve as a prime example of the lack of respect the wishes of Nevadans have received on this issue. On Valentine's Day, 2002, he recommended the project to President Bush. The next day, Bush signed off on Yucca—this after making a campaign promise to study the issue fairly and base his decision on science, not on politics. (It should be noted that the Environmental Impact Statement has not been conducted on Yucca, and the project's proponents and engineers have had to adjust their own safety and health regulations as the project has failed to meet tougher standards. In other words, the DOE has failed to play by its own rules and has been forced to rewrite them.)

To some, that Thursday, February 14 was the St. Valentine's Day Massacre revisited with Abraham wielding the tommy gun with his recommendation of Yucca Mountain as the nation's nuclear waste dump.

Rat-a-tat-tat.

To me, it was just another day in Nevada. Perhaps that Friday will become known as "Black Friday," after President Bush signed off on Abraham's recommendation, setting loose another barrage of angry sound bites from Nevada politicians.

The remarks of Democratic Senator and Majority Whip Harry Reid were the most scathing. He called Bush a liar who had betrayed the trust of all Nevadans who'd helped him win election. Reid and other Democrats surely were taking political advantage of the president's decision.

But was this really the second St. Valentine's Day Massacre and Black Friday, Part II?

No, just another couple of days in Nevada. Around these parts, you learn to live with the dirty looks and disrespect from Washington, the Bible Belt, and the whole damn nation during an election year. After a few years, you expect outsiders to treat the state with suspicion and disdain. You don't have to accept it, but there it is.

Yucca Mountain is another reminder that Nevada is not like other states. In the national respect department, Nevada has taken more lead than Dillinger. We make Rodney Dangerfield look loved.

Rat-a-tat-tat.

No one who has studied the national nuclear waste issue can argue that Yucca Mountain's 1987 selection as the sole study site was a fair one. They didn't call it the "Screw Nevada" bill for nothing. Nevada was selected not because it was deemed scientifically suitable, but because its small congressional delegation couldn't derail legislation backed by senators and representatives whose careers had been championed, and partially underwritten, by the nuclear power industry.

Once Yucca was selected and the government began pouring billions into it, the message was clear. Despite all assurances that the site would be approved only if found scientifically suitable and safe, there was no backup plan. The project's motto should have been: "2010 or bust."

While Nevada has gained a reputation for its honest games of chance, the DOE and nuclear industry have held most of the cards in the Yucca game for many years. Which makes it particularly irksome to hear pronuclear lobbyist John Sununu boast, "Most potent poisons last forever. This stuff doesn't." He knows that scientists believe the high-level nuclear waste planned for storage at Yucca will remain hazardous for at least 300,000 years. He also knows that, as governor of New Hampshire, he fought hard to have nuclear waste removed from his state for health, safety and political reasons. Spent fuel rods would have rested safely in his state's vast granite deposits, but he wouldn't hear of it. That was different. That was New Hampshire. This is Nevada.

Rat-a-tat-tat.

Outsiders and Nevada's Yucca supporters have argued for years that the dump, with its 77,000-ton capacity, was inevitable and it was unproductive and even damaging to the state's interests to continue to fight. Politicians who fight against it are accused of pandering, and others who flatly oppose it are labeled unreasonable, ill-informed and paranoid. It's in the middle of nowhere, they say. Nevada's population is low, they say. The state already has the test site, they say. You keep it, we shout. No, you take it, Abraham announced. Although Gov. Kenny Guinn has promised to oppose Abraham's recommendation, President Bush—whose relationship with Big Power is already the subject of journalistic investigation—brushed aside Nevada's plea for leniency. With few Nevada allies in Congress, the site is slated to open as early as 2010, but more likely by 2015. Projected cost: from $40 billion to as much as $58 billion.

So why not give in, as Yucca's allies suggest, and try to negotiate for benefits? Why not accept our new mantle as the nation's nuclear waste graveyard? Hey, maybe we can market it and make a buck, right? We can change the state's motto from "Battle Born" to "America Dumps on Us." We could do that, and maybe collect a federal stipend for our cooperation, or we can fight for the next decade. In that time, our clout in Congress can only improve. Senator Harry Reid and the rest of the delegation might collect enough political favors to generate hearings to address the propriety of the study process. In that time, Nevada will have a chance to fully explore its legal options. In that time, science and technology will have dramatically improved the odds of finding clean uses and on-site solutions for spent nuclear fuel and radioactive military garbage. And if we fail, at least we can tell our children that we tried. Perhaps by then the project's supporters will provide credible answers to a few basic questions: If it's so safe to transport, why isn't it safe to store in the states that produce it?

If there is a jackpot at Yucca Mountain, why not tell us how much? If the repository will employ many Nevadans, why are there no reliable estimates? There is no pot of gold buried at Yucca Mountain. Think about it: Would even $1 billion and a couple hundred jobs change the collective quality of life in a state with an annual general fund budget of $1.9 billion? What would one spill, and the resulting international news story, do to our tourism industry?

Nuclear waste is a volatile political issue in those states now reaching their storage capacity. They don't want it, and Nevada has been designated to relieve the pressure. Beyond the politics and even the science, there's the tattered image of a state already maligned more than most.

Most Las Vegans think it's worth fighting over.

19

State of the City

Only in Las Vegas could a former mob attorney turn the political establishment upside down by daring to run for mayor. But that's precisely what criminal defense lawyer Oscar Goodman did when he swept into office by a landslide in the spring of 1999.

Goodman bragged of his copious Beefeater gin consumption and sizable sports betting habit. He admitted he wasn't up on all the issues and concerns at the city. The fact was, he'd probably never been to a City Council meeting before and initially didn't realize that the city was run under a strong-manager form of government, which relegated the mayor's official duties to ribbon-cutting and a vote on the council. But Goodman had never let a few pesky facts get in the way of a good argument.

Truth was, his timing was ideal. The public, long since grown tired of the usual mediocre minds and tepid rhetoric, fell in love with his candor and his energy. He might not have known much about city politics, but most of the voters didn't care. Goodman, a University of Pennsylvania Law School graduate known nationally for his defense of under-world characters ranging from Meyer Lansky and Tony Spilotro to Nick Civella and Jimmy Chagra, immediately shook up City Hall and the political establishment throughout the state with his refresh-ingly blunt observations.

Not surprisingly, few of those observations were appreciated by the political mainstream—the same people who'd discounted his candidacy and claimed his election would set Las Vegas back 100 years. (Hey, the place wasn't even a century old.)

City Hall these days is defined by Goodman's character—both positively and negatively. His early boasts of bringing an NBA franchise and a sports arena to care-worn downtown were the words of a loose-lipped neophyte who was ignorant of the facts. (The NBA would never allow one of its teams in Las Vegas because of its legalized professional basketball sports betting.)

Goodman was used to getting his own way as the head of a law practice, and had grown accustomed in court to talking his way to victory. But the city faced a crisis not even the formidable rhetoric of

Oscar Goodman could overcome with mere words.

While the outer reaches of the city continued to expand with new residential neighborhoods and commercial development, the core of Las Vegas known as downtown was rapidly being abandoned by residents and businesses. The Fremont Street casinos were considered distant also-rans in the race for gambling dollars, and the colorful Fremont Street Experience light show was a blinking mediocrity.

Once he began to settle down, if only a little, Goodman set to work to secure 61-acres of undeveloped land on property downtown owned by the Union Pacific Railroad. With studies from the Urban Land Institute showing that downtown's only real hope for a renaissance would come with the development of a large piece of real estate, the 61 acres were the area's last best hope. Once the trade was made, Goodman's big talk of one day seeing an academic medical and research hospital downtown along with a performing arts center and, yes, eventually a big-league sports franchise, seemed almost believable.

Although the blight of downtown is still palpable, and the homeless problem threatens Goodman's legacy in large part due to his ill-advised outspokenness on the subject, there are signs that Las Vegans are beginning to see the inner urban core of the city the mayor's way.

Neighborhoods on the edge of downtown have begun to see a resurgence of young professionals. Several city redevelopment projects are in various stages of development. The changes are slight, and the long list of previous redevelopment flops would indicate that it doesn't pay to get too optimistic downtown, but where there is hope there is a chance that one day the streets that once defined early Las Vegas will once again be vibrant.

In late 2001, the Boyd Gaming Corp. closed a deal to develop a multipurpose sports arena of more than 5,000 seats to use as a minor-league hockey and convention venue on land previously used as a parking lot. The investment in downtown by a casino corporation was not only rare, but laudable. Some businessmen appeared to be buying into Goodman's energetic vision. It might not have been big league but it was movement in the right direction.

Overall, the key would appear to lie in the city's ability to accomplish small victories while planning for the potential home run of the 61 acres. Although Goodman is increasingly criticized for his broad-brush oral assaults on the gaming industry, which he's accused of not doing its part to revitalize downtown, (and that the gaming industry has been a nonplayer in the Yucca Mountain nuclear waste repository fight), his popularity with the voters remains high. If he continues to invest his time and energy, isn't distracted by talk of running for governor, and keeps a majority of City Council members in his camp, some of Goodman's lofty goals might be realized sooner than even he imagines.

20

Political Landscape: Money Talks

It's no secret. Money rules politics. In Washington, Congressmen grew boozy on Enron Corp. contributions while the company was hiding assets and setting investors up for one of the biggest corporate implosions in the nation's history.

While senators pay lip service to campaign finance reform, year after year little changes because the fact is money has always ruled politics. The wealthy's voice has always been heard over the cries of the poor, disadvantaged and downtrodden. The only real surprise in politics is that the working classes ever catch a break at all.

As goes the nation, so goes Nevada. In the Silver State, a few major influences exercise an enormous

control over the legislative process, but no industry—not even the traditional political powerhouses
of mining and ranching—have the clout of the casino industry. What it wants, with few exceptions, it
gets when the Legislature meets on alternate years
in the state capitol of Carson City.

Whether it's protecting its nation-low gaming
tax rate (6.25 percent), or carving out a juicy art tax
break for casino mogul Steve Wynn, the Legislature
is generally an obedient lapdog for the gamers. The
rebels and outspoken exceptions are generally mar-
ginalized by industry-friendly media as "loose can-
nons." Although a few survive, lobbyists ensure they
rarely are successful at making substantive change.

It's a Nevada tradition since the days a young
Mark Twain roamed the legislature and made this
inspired observation in his book *Roughing It* "In
Nevada, for a time, the lawyer, the editor, the
banker, the chief desperado, the chief gambler, and
the saloon-keeper, occupied the same level in society, and it was the highest. The cheapest and easiest
way to become an influential man and be looked up
to by the community at large, was to stand behind a
bar, wear a cluster-diamond pin, and sell whisky. I
am not sure but that the saloon-keeper held a shade
higher rank than any other member of society. His
opinion had weight. It was his privilege to say how
the elections should go. No great movement could
succeed without the countenance and direction of
the saloon-keepers. It was a high favor when the
chief saloon-keeper consented to serve in the legislature or the board of aldermen. Youthful ambition

hardly aspired so much to the honors of the law, or the army and navy as to the dignity of proprietorship in a saloon. To be a saloon-keeper and kill a man was to be illustrious."

More than a century later, saloon-keepers have evolved into casino operators, and they still rule the Legislature. "In Nevada, Democracy has been replaced by a Plutocracy with rich special interest donors (corporations and associations) selecting and funding candidates," the Progressive Leadership Alliance observed in its January 2002 report on the state of political finance. "Candidates are not accountable to the citizens of Nevada, but instead are beholden to their campaign contributors."

While some would argue the observation of PLAN's leadership, including Paul Brown and Bob Fulkerson, was too generalized, the group also backed up its assertion with a lengthy list of facts. Chief of which: with few exceptions, the best-funded candidate won, and the casino and development communities and large labor organizations were the biggest contributors to those candidates. Was it any wonder they nearly always received their wishes at the legislature? In 2000, legislators received a total of $7.62 million, a four percent increase over the previous session. (Incumbents out-raised opponents by more than a five-to-one margin.)

"Nearly 80 percent of the contributions went to incumbents," Brown and Fulkerson wrote in their report. "Many incumbent lawmakers faced only token opponents; some faced no opponent at all. Only one incumbent lost (she was outspent by her opponent). Fulkerson, PLAN's State Director, said, "Winning candidates and cash go together like caviar and champagne. On Election Day, voters did little more than rubber-stamp the choices made by the rich special interests—the Plutocrats."

Added Brown, PLAN's Southern Nevada Director, "Our system of special interest campaign financing is not working in the public interest. Special interests expect and get sweetheart deals and tax breaks for their campaign contributions."

Each of the state's 63 legislators is paid just $7,800 per session, but more than $7.6 million was raised. PLAN observed that given those numbers the contributions could pay the legislators' salaries for the next 31 years. Excluding political parties, labor actually outspent gaming in 2000, $985,288 to $885,228.

What did PLAN recommend? First, that the state set aside $5,000 per assembly and senate race to fund candidate debates to be aired on public television. Second, outlaw the post-election political contributions that built those obscene war chests. Third, raise lawmakers' pay so more can afford to serve. Last, to make campaign contribution reports available to candidates on computer disks.

With the exception of the last recommendation, PLAN's progressive views promised to be largely ignored by a state government under the spell of special interest. "A healthy representative government depends on a fully informed electorate and full exposure of the financial clout of the fat cats in the political process," Common

Cause/Nevada Chairman Jim Hulse said. But, as some longtime political observers have noted, even that won't appear to change the way business gets done in Carson City.

Epilogue

Outside Views: Hollywood and the Media

If you watch the movies, then you know the score. Vegas isn't a town, it's a virus. It's a deceit-stained dice pit lined with foul-mouthed mobsters, coked-up strippers, and booze-addled dreamers.

Every pass is snake eyes here in the land of the neon sun. The game is rigged. Sisyphus rolls these crooked dice time after time.

Even Dante would fear Vegas—at least the one portrayed on the big screen.

Las Vegas has long been a favorite setting for

Hollywood, but in the mid-1990s, the dark themes pouring forth from the city onto the screen were downright disturbing. From Martin Scorsese's mob epic *Casino*, Mike Figgis's darkly artistic Charter Hospital commercial *Leaving Las Vegas*, and Paul Verhoeven's unmentionable backhanded tribute to the city's silicone sisters *Showgirls*, you can understand what makes the squares at the Las Vegas Chamber of Commerce run for the Maalox. It's a wonder the phones at southern Nevada's Suicide Prevention Hotline don't ring off the hook.

The fact is, they sometimes do, but it's not the movies that concern Las Vegas residents. It's the reality of living in the fastest-growing community in America on the cusp of the twenty-first century that can take its toll on residents.

With few exceptions, the movies that pour forth from the city are awash in vice and blood, skinny girls and big guns. To Hollywood's directorial grifters, it's that kind of town. It's easy to see the city as the average tourist sees it: From the Strip to downtown, the joint is one lusty, seething big-budget movie set with the bright lights and dark magic built in.

But, unless you're playing, gambling is pretty boring. That's a big reason why, for all the dozens of movies that have been set in Las Vegas, so few of the good ones have anything to do with cards and dice. They're props; the characters are what make the city a case for study.

The characters were part of what used to make Las Vegas a great place to live. This place ought to have been Runyon's winter home. The guys and dolls not only hung out in the casinos, but they also shopped at the Safeway and lived in quiet neighborhoods and sent their kids to school here.

Most of that has changed. With more than 1 million people living in the metropolitan area—and the population expected to double in a decade—Las Vegas isn't just a surrealistic roadside rest stop anymore. With more than 30 million visitors converging on the city—and $5.7 billion in gaming revenue generated countywide—the city rivals Disney World as the nation's top tourist destination.

Problem is, Las Vegas has not yet emerged from intense therapy. It's made strides, but still suffers from an inferiority complex and all-world growing pains. Problem is, Las Vegas is not just like every other maturing metropolis. The casino lifestyle has something to do with it, but many of the problems are attributable to a single factor.

It's the growth. Las Vegas is America's last great boomtown, and the casinos comprise the Comstock Lode. The city perennially ranks at or near the top of the fastest-growing category. That's good news for developers, who have built thousands of houses and apartments to accommodate the legions of monied retirees and short-pockets service workers who have invaded in Joad family fashion in search of good jobs and warm winters.

That's the Las Vegas story. It's not as lascivious as *Showgirls* or as bloody as *Casino*, but growth—with all its blessings and curses—is the greater reality around these parts.

Nevada led the nation last year in personal-income growth and ranks ninth in per-capita income. In 1995, nearly 19,500 homes were built in the valley to accommodate the four thousand people who move here each month. That's the good news.

The state leads the nation in other categories as well. Crime, for instance. Nevada topped the country with a 13 percent increase in 1994, according to the FBI's annual report.

But all this success may be toughest on the children: highest teen suicide rate, second highest teen pregnancy rate. Nevada is last in the nation in aid to preschool children and has the fourth-highest teen-death rate and the highest juvenile incarceration rate in America. It also has the highest high school dropout rate in America.

The state also leads the nation in alcohol consumption and smoking, and the Las Vegas valley battles a lack of public parks and an air quality problem that ranks it among the country's worst cities.

The dilemma in education might be the greatest problem facing southern Nevada's future. The state's libertarian, laissez-faire business philosophy simply does not fit the vast needs of the population. The children of the boom are suffering, and it's something all newcomers to southern Nevada must consider. Former Clark County School District Superintendent Brian Cram was not exaggerating when he told community leaders that education is about opening doors and not about closing cell doors behind troubled teenagers.

There's an element of truth to the Hollywood image of Las Vegas as the mob's final frat house, Figgis's booze hell, and even Verhoeven's floozy fest. Its noir elements are seductive, and not only to tourists and movie producers. People really do get lost here.

It's also a place for second chances, the kind working people are willing to live and die and travel 3,000 miles to find. No one can blame Hollywood for missing the real Las Vegas story, but the growing pains of the nation's last great boomtown are no less compelling than any dark image drawn by Scorsese.

When you move to Las Vegas, you learn to accept the dark with the light.

Appendix

Fifty Las Vegans You Should Know

Former Mayor Jan Jones

The city's first woman mayor, Jones is a former automobile dealership executive who ran an unsuccessful race for governor. She is currently an executive with the Harrah's casino corporation.

Bob Stupak

The former Vegas World Casino owner defines the word flamboyant. He dreamed up the idea for the 1,149-foot Stratosphere Tower, paid a man to jump off the top of his twenty-two-story hotel, once won a $1-million bet on the Super Bowl, and survived more than one state Gaming Control Board inquiry into his business practices. He is the subject of the biography *No Limit* by John L. Smith.

J. Terrence "Terry" Lanni

He's the Chairman of MGM Mirage, operators of the MGM Grand, Mirage, Bellagio, Treasure Island and other resorts. Considered a leading force in the gaming industry.

Frank Fahrenkopf

He directs the American Gaming Association, the casino industry's lobbying and strategy arm.

Steve Wynn

With wildly successful resorts, a formidable political machine, and a willingness to force his will on elected officials, until early 2000 Wynn was the reigning king of Las Vegas. Wynn's feuds with Atlantic City gaming figure Donald Trump as well as his increased interest in national issues and presidential politics dramatically increased his public profile. But that didn't prevent Wynn's Mirage Resorts from being purchased by Kirk Kerkorian's MGM Grand. The company is now called MGM Mirage. Wynn is the subject of the 1995 investigative biography, *Running Scared: The Life and Treacherous Times of Las Vegas Casino King Steve Wynn* written by John L. Smith and published by Barricade Books.

Harry Reid

Born in Searchlight, Harry Reid is a southern

Nevada success story. Overcoming a poor upbringing, Reid traveled 160 miles a day to and from high school, and now he is the second most powerful Democrat in the U.S. Senate.

Richard Bryan

The former U.S. senator remains a fierce opponent of the federal government's attempt to put a nuclear waste repository at Yucca Mountain in central Nevada. Bryan distinguished himself as a staunch advocate of his constituents. The Democrat was raised locally and worked in the Clark County Public Defender and District Attorney's offices.

Andre Agassi

The champion professional tennis player not only is a longtime Las Vegan, but also makes a substantial contribution to the community through the Andre Agassi Foundation.

Greg Maddux

The Valley High graduate is the Cy Young Award-winning pitcher for the Atlanta Braves and one of many Las Vegans to make a mark in professional sports.

John Ensign

The stepson of Circus Circus executive Mike Ensign, John burst onto the political scene in 1994 when he upset incumbent James Bilbray to win one of Nevada's two seats in the House of

Representatives. The Republican is now a U.S. Senator.

Dr. Carol Harter

UNLV's president took over for the embattled Robert Maxson, whose tenure was highlighted by unprecedented growth at the state university but also was marred by a nasty fight with legendary Runnin' Rebels basketball coach Jerry Tarkanian.

Bill Hanlon

The longtime math instructor not only teaches arithmetic at all levels; he also writes an education column and conducts televised lessons on the local public station.

Carlos Garcia

The superintendent of the Clark County School District has the difficult task of guiding K-12 education in a boomtown.

Kirk Kerkorian

The quiet billionaire, who is responsible for building the largest hotel in the world three times during his thirty-year Las Vegas tenure, often is sighted at local restaurants dining in near-anonymity. These days, he spends more of his time in Los Angeles.

Jerry Keller

Clark County's former sheriff is a Western High

graduate who ascended the ranks of the Metropolitan Police Department and defeated venerable ex-sheriff Ralph Lamb for the job.

Bill Young

The Metro police veteran replaced Keller as sheriff in 2002. A family man, Young is a 23-year police veteran.

Bob Broadbent

As the executive director of McCarran International Airport, Broadbent shepherded the growth of the airport, one of the busiest and most efficient in America.

Bill Branon

He is a popular local writer whose novels include *Let Us Prey* and *Devil's Hole.*

Sherman Frederick

As the publisher of the *Las Vegas Review-Journal,* Nevada's largest newspaper, Frederick carries substantial political clout and now is a major executive with the Stephens Media Group.

Sig Rogich

The longtime political power player is a former member of Reagan and first Bush administrations' inner circles. He is a top advisor to Republicans and some Democrats and very close with Gov. Kenny Guinn.

Kenny Guinn

The popular Republican Governor is the former superintendent of schools and a retired corporate executive.

Dina Titus

The UNLV political science professor and author leads Democrats in the state senate.

Patricia Mulroy

As the executive director of the Las Vegas Water Authority and head of the Las Vegas Valley Water District, Mulroy is one of the most powerful figures in the state.

Brian Greenspun

The eldest son of late *Las Vegas Sun* publisher Hank Greenspun, Brian is an attorney who heads his family's publishing, cable television, and development dynasty. As a former classmate of Bill Clinton, Greenspun played an active role in communicating the interests of Nevadans and the casino industry to the White House during the Democrat's administration.

Jackie Gaughan

Patriarch of the Gaughan gambling family, whose local casinos include the Barbary Coast and son Michael Gaughan's Gold Coast, Jackie Gaughan arrived in Las Vegas in 1946 and now owns six downtown casinos.

Oscar Goodman

The mob lawyer-turned-mayor of Las Vegas remains popular with voters and is often mentioned for higher office.

Larry Brown

The Las Vegas City Councilman is a Harvard graduate and former minor-league pitcher.

Gary Reese

The Mayor Pro-Tem of Las Vegas is a full-time barber.

Lawrence Weekly

The Las Vegas City Councilman is a former city constituent liaison and is a local success story, rising from humble economic means to City Hall.

Michael McDonald

The Las Vegas City Councilman is a former Metro police officer.

Lynette Boggs McDonald

The Las Vegas City Councilwoman is a Notre Dame graduate and ran unsuccessfully for Congress in 2002.

Billy Vassiliadis

The head of R&R Partners Advertising is perhaps the most trusted political advisor in the state.

Jim Ferrence

The political advisor was a key behind-the-scenes player in the surprise election of Oscar Goodman.

Randy Black

The developer, who owns casinos in Mesquite, is an important player in Republican Party politics.

Kent Oram

The longtime political advisor has rarely lost a campaign.

Bill Bible

The former Chairman of the Gaming Control Board and current leader of the Nevada Resort Association.

Virginia Valentine

The former Las Vegas City Manager is now a political strategist for the Las Vegas Chamber of Commerce.

Thom Reilly

The Clark County manager.

Erin Kenny

Clark County Commissioner. A Democrat.

Dario Herrera

Chairman of the Clark County Commission and a candidate for Congress in 2002. A Democrat.

Myrna Williams

Clark County Commissioner and former longtime member of the Nevada Assembly. A Democrat.

Yvonne Atkinson Gates

Clark County Commissioner. Often mentioned as a candidate for higher office. A Democrat and the first black female commissioner.

Chip Maxfield

First-term County Commissioner. A Republican.

Bill Walters

Professional sports bettor and golf course developer.

Michael Montandon

The mayor of North Las Vegas.

Jim Gibbons

The Henderson mayor is mentioned consistently as a potential candidate for higher office.

Brian Cram

The former Clark County School District Superintendent works as an education consultant to the Greenspun family's foundation.

Richard Perkins

The Henderson police officer is the Speaker of the State Assembly. A Democrat.

Bruce Woodbury

Longtime County Commissioner and resident of Boulder City. Known as the most stable force on an often volatile commission.

Jim Rogers

Owner of KVBC TV-3, the local NBC affiliate, he's a lawyer, a generous contributor to UNLV and an outspoken editorialist.

Gary Gray

A longtime Democratic Party political advisor and campaign manager. Married to Assemblywoman Chris Giunchigliani.

Hal Rothman

UNLV professor of history and author of several books on the growth of Las Vegas.

Appendix

25 Dates in Las Vegas History

11,000 BC	Near the site of Las Vegas, human beings live and hunt
1843 AD	John C. Fremont begins mapping territory that would become Nevada
1855	Mormon missionaries open a mission in Las Vegas
1857	Mormon missionaries close their mission in Las Vegas
1864	Nevada admitted to Union as the thirty-sixth state
1905	Las Vegas becomes a town site
1911	Las Vegas officially becomes a city

1931	Governor signs six-week divorce law
1931	Gambling legalized in Nevada
1941	The first resort on the Las Vegas Strip—the El Rancho—opens; the El Cortez opens downtown
1946	Ben Siegel's Flamingo opens
1947	Ben Siegel murdered in Beverly Hills
1950	The Desert Inn opens
1951	First atomic weapon tested at Nevada Test Site; Benny Binion opens the Horseshoe Club
1952	The Sands and Sahara open
1954	The Showboat opens
1955	The Dunes and Riviera open
1957	Nevada Southern University (now University of Nevada, Las Vegas) erects its first permanent building
1958	Las Vegas Convention Center opens
1963	McCarran Airport opens
1966	Caesars Palace opens
1968	Circus Circus opens
1969	International Hotel (now the Las Vegas Hilton) opens
1973	MGM Grand (now Bally's) opens
1995	Landmark Hotel demolished to create additional parking for Las Vegas Convention Center

Appendix

Ten Las Vegans From the Past

William Clark

The Montana senator's railroad went through southern Nevada in the early twentieth century and led to the development of Las Vegas as a city.

Benjamin "Bugsy" Siegel

The best-known, and perhaps most overrated, influence on Las Vegas, Siegel was murdered at the Beverly Hills home of galpal Virginia Hill in June 1947. Siegel is credited, wrongly, with the idea for the Flamingo Hotel. No one called him Bugsy while he was alive without regretting it.

Moe Dalitz

One of the founding fathers of the real Las Vegas, Dalitz was a Cleveland bootlegger with strong ties to Jimmy Hoffa's Teamsters Central States Pension Fund, who nevertheless migrated to Las Vegas and built not only casinos but hospitals and shopping malls as well. One of the great influences in Las Vegas history.

Gus Greenbaum

The man who took over for Benny Siegel met an equally violent demise in 1955, when killers cut his throat and that of his wife.

Benny Binion

The patriarch of the Binion's Horseshoe Club casino family, Benny was a Dallas rackets boss who admitted killing several men before coming to Las Vegas, where cards and dice were legal. A statue of Binion on horseback graces downtown.

Jay Sarno

The big-idea man behind Caesars Palace and Circus Circus, Sarno was one of the grandest, and least known, entrepreneurs in the history of the city.

Grant Sawyer

Perhaps Nevada's most important governor, Sawyer's political expertise guided the gaming industry away from federal scrutiny and toward state regulation.

Tony Cornero

This gambling boss operated casino ships off California and came to Las Vegas with a dream of building what became known as the Stardust. Cornero ran out of money and friends, and ended up dying of a heart attack at a Desert Inn craps table.

Howard Hughes

The eccentric billionaire occupied the ninth floor of the Desert Inn Hotel and bought seven casinos, but today his greatest impact is felt in the planned community developments at Summerlin in the northwest section of the valley.

Rex Bell, Sr.

The former Nevada lieutenant governor was married to silent-movie star Clara Bow. The Bell family once had a ranch near Nipton, California, close to the Nevada state line called the Walking Box.

Appendix

Twenty Nevada Facts

* Largest city in Nevada: Las Vegas; next largest, Reno.
* Population growth rate from 1980 to 1990: 50.38 percent.
* Nevada's area is 110,540 square miles.
* Nevada ranks seventh in state size.
* Halloween is a state holiday in Nevada because it happens to fall on its date of admission to the Union: October 31, 1864.
* Median age: 34.2.
* Population: 1,900,000.
* Nevada was once part of the Republic of Mexico. It was ceded to the United States in 1848 as part of the Treaty of Guadalupe Hidalgo.

* Amount of Nevada land federally-owned: 83 percent.
* Highest point: Boundary Peak in Esmeralda County–13,143 feet.
* State bird: mountain bluebird.
* State flower: shrub sagebrush.
* State tree: single-leaf pinion pine; also bristlecone pine.
* State motto: "All for our country."
* State nicknames: Silver State; Sagebrush State; Battle Born State (it became a state during the Civil War).
* State animal: bighorn sheep.
* State song: "Home Means Nevada" by Bertha Raffetto.
* State fish: Lahonton cutthroat trout.
* State reptile: desert tortoise.
* State rock: sandstone.
* State grass: Indian rice grass.
* State metal: silver.

Appendix

Helpful Las Vegas Websites

For those of you who surf the web, limitless information is available about Las Vegas. It takes some time and effort, but you can find the specific information you need if you keep at it. Here are some sites we find very helpful.

lvrj.com
This website, hosted by the *Las Vegas Review-Journal,* is a link to not just the local newspaper (which is entirely searchable for free) but to the whole community. Find information on daily events, shows, recreation, tv listings, community happenings, and tons of links to other community sites. Check out the "community links," where the *Review-Journal*

gives free site space to nonprofit organizations in town.

LasVegas.com
Any event–from today to next year–you will find on this site. Also, find listings for local movies, local government, recreation, places to visit, you name it. Locals use this site constantly to keep on top of happenings.

Move to LasVegas.com
A very handy site for those planning a move to Las Vegas. Its searchable form is very user-friendly and allows you to search for real estate agents, local businesses by type, apartments, utility information, job search information–just the things the new resident might need.

Jewishvegas.com
Laugh if you wish, but if you are Jewish and planning to move to Las Vegas, you will not find a more helpful site. It lists good delis, "where the Jewish people live," social information, clubs, religious organizations–many helpful pieces of information you might otherwise take lots of time to gather.

Lasvegas.about.com/cs/
A GREAT site which covers all the general info you might need about moving to Las Vegas, plus more specialized things–i.e., gay/lesbian info, art, health care, music, and dining. You will want to spend some time here to gather some tips of special interest to you.

Lvol.com

Called "Las Vegas Online," this site covers all the entertainment available. Find your way around town, look up shopping centers, search for local businesses, plus MUCH more.

Intermind.net/im/lasvegas.html

Although this site is a bit tourist-oriented, there is helpful information here, such as "100 things to do in Las Vegas," plus weather, current movie listings, and shopping info.

Vegasinfo.com

Another good all-around site, especially if you click on the "jobs" section. Here you will find listings of all casino and government jobs, links to the Nevada Employment Department, plus click to get a free newsletter about jobs in Las Vegas. Extremely helpful for those searching for a job.

Appendix

Las Vegas New Home Builders

If you are in the market to purchase a new home, you may want to contact some builders before you move. Most of the builders will be happy to send you brochures and maps showing the various neighborhoods they have built.

American Premiere Homes
235 W. Brooks Avenue N.
Las Vegas, NV 89030
702-399-6137

AmLand Development, Inc.
7140 Industrial Road, Suite 1200
Las Vegas, NV 89118
702-870-5772

Astoria Homes
2500 West Sahara Ave., Suite 206
Las Vegas, NV 89102
702-257-1188

Beazer Homes Nevada Inc.
770 E. Warm Springs Rd.
Las Vegas, NV 89119
702-837-2100
This builder has become very popular in all areas of town and all price ranges.

Capital Pacific Homes
3200 Soaring Gulls Dr.
Las Vegas, NV 89128
702-362-2000

Carina Corporation
2881 Business Park Court #210
Las Vegas, NV 89128
702-228-6376

Chartered Homes
7120 W. Tropicana Ave.
Las Vegas, NV 89103
702-873-3994

Coleman Homes
1635 Village Center Ct.
Las Vegas, NV 89134
702-243-9800

Concordia Homes of Nevada, Inc.
6360 South Pecos Road, Suite G
Las Vegas, NV 89120
702-434-5200
This builder makes particularly nice, spacious homes with many extras not included by some other builders.

Developers Of Nevada
7448 West Sahara Ave.
Las Vegas, NV 89117
702-221-1410
888-250-7033

Emerald Development
Semi-Custom Home Builders
4005 Villa Flora
Las Vegas, NV 89130
702-396-6782

Falcon Homes Inc.
2280 S. Jones
Las Vegas, NV 89102
702-871-6677

Kaufman & Broad Of Nevada
4755 Industrial Rd.
Las Vegas, NV 89103
702-261-1300
800-34-HOMES
Another one of the Las Vegas "biggies." Many neighborhoods
bear this company's name, in various price ranges, but all with
a nice touch.

Lewis Homes Of Nevada
3325 Ali Baba Lane
Las Vegas, NV 89118
702-736-8960
Lewis Homes has been here for decades and has a proven track
record of quality products.

Pacific Homes
3111 S. Maryland Pkwy.
Las Vegas, NV 89109
702-735-0191

Pardee Homes
4835 S. Rainbow Blvd.
Las Vegas, NV 89103
702-876-2634
888-4-PARDEE
Another "oldie but goodie." Pardee is still making beautiful homes at affordable prices.

Perennial Homes
5440 West Sahara Ave., Third Floor
Las Vegas, NV 89102
702-221-1111

Primack Homes
1900 Grey Eagle Street
Henderson, NV 89014
702-260-6707

Pulte Homes
1635 Village Center Circle
Las Vegas, NV 89134
702-256-7900
800-GO-PULTE

Real Homes By Centex Homes
3600 N. Rancho Dr.
Las Vegas, NV 89130
Real Homes by Centex Homes has been building in CA & NV for over 20 years.

Rhodes Homes
4630 Arville St.
Las Vegas, NV 89103
702-873-5338

Stanpark Homes Of Nevada
3320 N. Buffalo Dr.
Las Vegas, NV 89129
702-396-3887
We have toured this builder's houses and found them well-constructed and nicely thought out.

Watt Homes - Nevada
1601 S. Rainbow Blvd., Suite 160
Las Vegas, NV 89102
702-256-2323

Westpoint Development Group, Inc.
3930 W. Ali Baba Lane
Las Vegas, NV 89118
702-739-9033
Builders of Quality Custom Homes and Commercial projects since 1988.

Wexford Homes
2260 Corporate Circle
Henderson, NV 89014
702-454-5300
Experience, dedication to excellence, and a true concern for each and every home.

Appendix

Parks and Sports Facilities

For more information, contact these city and county departments:

Las Vegas Parks and Leisure
702-229-6571

North Las Vegas Parks & Recreation Department
702-633-1177

Henderson Recreation Department
702-565-2063

Boulder City Recreation Department
702-293-9256

Clark County Parks & Recreation Department
702-455-8200

LAS VEGAS PARKS

NW = northwest Las Vegas
SW = southwest Las Vegas
NE = northeast Las Vegas
SE = southeast Las Vegas
C = central Las Vegas

Aloha Shore
NW
Buffalo & Cheyenne
Picnic areas, playground,
restrooms, tennis, volleyball

Angel
NW
Westcliff & Durango
Picnic areas, playground,
restrooms, tennis

An San Sister
NW
Ducharme & Villa Monterey
Picnic area, playground,
restrooms, volleyball

Baker
SE
St. Louis & 10th
Ball fields, basketball, picnic
areas, playground, tennis

Bob Baskin
C
Rancho & Oakey
Picnic areas, playground,
restrooms, tennis, water play

Bruce Trent
NW
Rampart & Vegas
Picnic areas, playground,
restrooms, tennis

Bucskin Basin
NW
Tenaya & Gowan
Playground

Charleston Heights
NW
Smoke Ranch & Maverick
Ball fields, picnic areas, play-
ground, volleyball

Charleston Neighborhood
Preservation
NW
I-95 & Torrey Pines
Ball fields, picnic areas, play-
ground

Chester Stupak
C
Boston & Fairfield
Basketball, picnic areas, play-
ground

Children's Memorial
NW
Torrey Pines & Gowan
Ball fields, picnic areas, play-ground, restrooms

Cimmaron Range
NW
Ann & Cimmaron
Picnic areas, restrooms

Clarence Ray Memorial
C
Tonopah & Washington
Picnic areas, playground, restrooms

Coleman
NW
Daybreak & Carmen
Playground

Cragin
C
Fulton & Hinson
Ball fields, playground, restrooms, pool, tennis

Dexter
C
Upland & Trent
Ball fields, basketball, picnic areas, playground, restrooms, tennis

Doolittle
C
Lake Mead & J
Ball fields, basketball, picnic areas, playground, restrooms, pool

Ed Fountain
C
Vegas & Decatur
Ball fields, picnic areas, play-ground, restrooms

Ethel Pearson
C
Washington & D
Picnic areas, playground, tennis

Fitzgerald Tot Lot
C
H & Monroe
Picnic areas, playground

Freedom
NE
Mojave & Washington
Ball fields, picnic areas, play-ground, restrooms, volleyball

Hadland
SE
28th & Stewart
Ball fields, picnic areas, play-ground, restrooms, pool

Heers
NW
Smoke Ranch & Zorro

Heritage
C
LV Blvd. & Washington
Picnic areas, restrooms

Hills
NW
Hillpointe Dr.
Ball fields, basketball, picnic areas, playground, restrooms, tennis, volleyball, water play

Huntridge Circle
C
Maryland Pkwy. & Franklin

James Gay III
NE
Owens & B
Basketball, picnic areas, playground

Jaycee
SE
St. Louis & Eastern
Ball fields, basketball, picnic areas, playground, restrooms, tennis

Lorenzi
C
Washington & Twin Lakes
Ball fields, basketball, picnic areas, playground, restrooms, tennis

Lubertha Johnson
NE
Balzar Ave. & Concord St.
Picnic areas, playground

Mary Dutton
C
Charleston & 10th St.
Playground

Mirabelli
NW
6200 Elton Ave.
Basketball, picnic areas, playground

Mountain Ridge
NW
Elkhorn & Durango
Ball fields, picnic areas

Pueblo
NW
Lake Mead Blvd. W. of Tenaya
Basketball, picnic areas, playground, restrooms

Rafael Rivera
SE
Stewart & Mojave
Ball fields, basketball, picnic areas, playground, restrooms, tennis, volleyball

Rainbow Family
SW
Oakey Blvd. W of Rainbow
Ball fields, picnic areas, playground, restrooms, water play

Rotary
C
Charleston & Hinson
Picnic areas, playground, restrooms

Stewart Place
NE
Marion & Chantilly
Playground

W. Charleston Lions
C
Essex Dr.
Picnic areas, playground, volleyball

W. Wayne Bunker
Tenaya & Alexander
Picnic areas, playground, restrooms, tennis, volleyball, running track

Wildwood
NW
Shadow Mtn. & Wildwood
Basketball, picnic areas, playground

Woofter Family
NW
Rock Springs & Vegas
Ball fields, picnic areas, playground, restrooms

NORTH LAS VEGAS PARKS

Antonello School
1101 W. Tropical Way
Ball fields

Borris Terrace
2200 E. Cartier
Basketball, picnic areas, playground

Brooks Tot Lot
1421 Brooks Ave.
Playground

Cheyenne Ridge
3814 Scott Robinson Dr.
Basketball, picnic areas, playground, volleyball

Cheyenne Sports Complex
3500 E. Cheyenne Ave.
Ball fields, restrooms, tennis

City View
101 Cheyenne Ave.
Picnic areas, playground, restrooms

College
2613 Tonapah Ave.
Picnic areas, playground

Eldorado
5900 Camino Eldorado
Picnic areas, playground

Flores
4133 Allen Ln.
Picnic areas, playground

Gold Crest
714 W. Craig Creek Ave.
Picnic areas, playground, restrooms, volleyball

Goynes
3909 W. Washington
Ball fields, picnic areas, playground, restrooms, volleyball

Hebert Memorial
2701 Basswood Ave.
Ball fields, picnic areas, playground, restrooms

Joe Kneip
2127 McCarran St.
Picnic areas, playground,
restrooms, tennis

Monte Vista
4910 Scott Robinson Dr.
Picnic areas, playground

Petitti
2505 N. Bruce St.
Ball fields, basketball, picnic
areas, playground, restrooms,
pool

Richard Tom
4631 Rockpine Dr.
Ball fields, basketball, picnic
areas, playground, restrooms,
pool

Rotary Tot Lot
2600 Magnet St.
Playground

Tom Williams School
1844 Belmont St.
Ball fields, basketball, picnic
areas

Tonopah
204 E. Tonopah
Basketball, picnic areas, play-
ground

Valley View
2000 Bennett St.
Ball fields, basketball, picnic
areas, playground

Walker
2227 W. Evans Ave.
Ball fields, basketball, picnic
areas, playground, volleyball

Walker Pool & Park
1509 June Ave.
Basketball, picnic areas, play-
ground, pool

HENDERSON PARKS

Allegro
1023 Seven Hills Blvd.
Ball fields, picnic areas, play-
ground, restrooms

Arroyo Grande
298 Arroyo Grande Blvd.
Ball fields, basketball, picnic
areas, playground, restrooms

Black Mtn.
599 Greenway Road
Restrooms, pool, tennis

BMI Park/Pool
105 Basic
Picnic areas, playground,
restrooms, pool

Burkholder
645 W. Victory Rd.
Ball fields, picnic areas, play-
ground, restrooms

Discovery
2011 Paseo Verde Pkwy.
Ball fields, basketball, picnic
areas, playground, restrooms,
tennis, volleyball

Fox Ridge
420 Valle Verde Rd.
Basketball, picnic areas, play-
ground, restrooms

Green Valley
370 N. Pecos Rd.
Ball fields, basketball, picnic
areas, playground, restrooms

McCall School
57 Lynn Road
Ball fields, picnic areas, play-
ground

Mission Hills
551 E. Mission Dr.
Ball fields, basketball, picnic
areas, playground, restrooms,
tennis

Morrell
500 Harris St.
Ball fields, basketball, picnic
areas, playground, restrooms,
tennis, volleyball

Mountain View
1959 Wigwam Pkwy.
Ball fields, basketball, picnic
areas, playground, restrooms,
tennis, volleyball

O'Callaghan
601 Skyline Rd.
Ball fields, basketball, picnic
areas, playground, restrooms,
tennis

Paseo Verde
1851 Paseo Verde Pkwy.
Ball fields, basketball, picnic
areas, playground, restrooms,
tennis, volleyball

Pecos Legacy
150 Pecos Rd.
Ball fields, basketball, picnic
areas, playground, restrooms,
tennis, volleyball

Paccini
1899 Seven Hills Dr.
Basketball, picnic areas, play-
ground, restrooms, tennis, vol-
leyball

River Mountain
1941 Appaloosa Rd.
Ball fields, basketball, picnic
areas, playground, restrooms,
tennis, volleyball

Roadrunner
831 Amigo Street
Picnic areas, playground

Rodeo
810 Aspen Peak
Ball fields, basketball, picnic
areas, playground, restrooms,
tennis, volleyball

Sewell School
700 E. Lake Mead Dr.
Ball fields, picnic areas, play-
ground

Sonata
1550 Seven Hills Drive
Picnic areas, playground,
restrooms

Stephanie Lynn Craig
1725 Galleria Dr.
Ball fields, picnic areas,
restrooms

Sundridge
1010 Sandy Ridge
Ball fields, basketball, picnic
areas, playground, restrooms,
tennis, volleyball

Titanium Field
88 Lake Mead Dr.
Ball fields, picnic areas

Trail Cyn
1065 Trail Canyon
Basketball, picnic areas, play-
ground, restrooms, tennis

Wells
Hollick Ave. and Price St.
Ball fields, basketball, picnic
areas, playground, restrooms,
pool, tennis, volleyball

White School
1661 Galleria Dr.
Ball fields, basketball, picnic
areas, playground, tennis, vol-
leyball

Vivaldi
1249 Seven Hills Drive
Ball fields, basketball, picnic
areas, playground, restrooms,
tennis, volleyball

BOULDER CITY PARKS

Bicentennial
Utah and Colorado
Picnic areas, playground

Boulder City
Swim/Racquetball Complex
861 Avenue B
Basketball, restrooms, volleyball

Bravo Softball Field
Avenue B
Restrooms, pool

Central
5th Street and Avenue B
Picnic areas, playground,
restrooms, pool, tennis, volley-
ball

Del Prado
Utah and Northridge
Basketball, picnic areas, play-
ground, volleyball

Frank T. Crowe Memorial
Birch and Cherry
Picnic areas

Hemenway Valley
Ville Dr.
Ball fields, basketball, picnic areas, playground, restrooms, tennis, volleyball

Lakeview
Walkey Way and Pyramid Lane
Basketball, picnic areas, playground

Oasis
Sandra Drive
Ball fields, basketball, picnic areas, playground, volleyball

River Mountain Hiking Trail
Adjacent to St. Jude's
Picnic areas

Veterans Memorial
Buchanan and Airport Rd.
Picnic areas, volleyball

Whalen Baseball and Softball
Avenue B
Ball fields, restrooms

CLARK COUNTY PARKS

Cannon School Park
SE
5850 Euclid
Ball fields, multi-use fields

Cashman School Park
SE
4622 W. Desert Inn Rd.

Davis Park
SW
2796 Redwood St.
Picnic areas and playgrounds

Desert Bloom Park
SE
8405 S. Maryland Parkway
Ball fields, basketball, picnic areas, playground, restrooms, pool, community center

Desert Breeze Park
SW
8425 Spring Mountain Rd.
Ball fields, basketball, picnic areas, playground, restrooms, pool, dog park, roller hockey and skateboarding

Desert Inn Mobile Estates Park
SE
3570 Vista Del Monte
Picnic areas, playground, pool, tee-ball field, walking paths, dog run

Dog Fancier's Park
SE
5800 E. Flamingo Rd.
Lighted dog run facility, water access, shade, restrooms

Durango School Park
7100 W. Dewey Dr.
SW
Ball fields

Eldorado School Park
NE
1139 N. Linn Ln.
Ball fields

Government Center Grounds
C
500 Grand Central Pkwy.
Grass performance
area/amphitheater

Guinn School
SW
6480 Fairbanks Rd.
Ball fields, basketball, tennis,
volleyball, community center,
restrooms

Harmony Park
SE
Harmon and Pearl
Playground, picnic areas,
walking track, fitness course

Hidden Palms Park
SE
8855 Hidden Palms Pkwy.
Playground, picnic areas, bas-
ketball, tennis, volleyball, fit-
ness course

Horseman's Park
SE
5800 E. Flamingo Rd.
Picnic area, restrooms, arena
seating, two arenas, 320 stalls

Laurelwood
SE
4300 Newcastle Rd.
Playground, picnic areas,
restrooms, basketball, tennis
court, jogging trail

Lewis Family
SW
1970 Tree Line Dr.
Picnic areas, playground,
restrooms, tennis court, basket-
ball, jogging trail

Lone Mountain
NW
4445 N. Jensen
Picnic areas, playground,
restrooms, tennis, volleyball,
jogging trail, sand volleyball
court, roller hockey/skateboard-
ing

Lynnwood
2646 Lynwood Street
Picnic area, playground

Magdalena's Vegas Mountain
SE
4580 Vegas Valley Drive
Playground

Martin Luther King Park
NE
5439 E. Carey
Picnic area, basketball, walk-
ing track

Maslow Park
NE
4900 Lana Dr.
Ball fields, multi-use fields, picnic areas, playground, walking/jogging path, restrooms, pool, tennis

Paul Meyer Park &
Community Center
SW
4525 New Forest Dr.
Ball fields, picnic areas, playground, tennis

Mountain Crest Park
NW
4701 N. Durango
Multiuse fields, picnic areas, restrooms, playground, walking trail, disc golf course, horseshoe court

Mountain View School Park
NW
5436 E. Kell Ln.
Ball field, tee-ball field

Nellis Meadows Park
NE
4949 E. Cheyenne Ave.
Ball fields, picnic areas, playground, restrooms, sand volleyball, BMX track, multiuse fields

Orr School Park
SE
1520 E. Katie
Picnic areas, playground, ball fields, tennis, multiuse fields

Paradise Park & Community
Center
SE
4770 S. Harrison Dr.
Ball field, basketball, playground, picnic areas, restrooms, pool, tennis, fitness course

Paradise Vista Park
SE
5582 Stirrup St.
Picnic areas, playground, multiuse fields, horseshoe pit

Parkdale Park & Community
Center
SE
3200 Ferndale St.
Playground, picnic areas, restrooms, basketball, pool, senior wing

Potosi Park
SW
2750 Mohawk
Ball fields, picnic area, restrooms

Prosperity Park
7101 Parasol Ln.
Ball fields, basketball, picnic area, playground, walking-jogging trail

Shadow Rock Park
2650 Los Feliz
Softball fields, picnic areas,
playground, dog run

Silverado Ranch Park
SE
9855 Gillespie St.
Ball fields, picnic areas, barbe-
cue areas, playground, skate
park, walking track, amphithe-
ater

Silvestri School Park
SW
1055 E. Silverado Ranch
Blvd.
Ball field, multiuse field

Southern Nevada Vocational
Technical Center
SE
Ball fields, multiuse field

Spring Valley Park
SW
4220 Ravenwood Dr.
Ball fields, playground, basket-
ball

Sunrise Park and Community
Center
SE
2240 Linn Ln.
Ball fields, picnic areas, play-
ground, restrooms, pools, ten-
nis, basketball

Sunset Park and Lake
SE
2601 E. Sunset Rd.
Ball fields, picnic areas, play-
ground, restrooms, pool, tennis,
volleyball, basketball, fitness
course, walking-jogging track,
disc golf courts, horseshoe pits,
multiuse fields, radio con-
trolled boating, dog run

Von Tobel Park
NE
3610 E. Carey
Ball fields, picnic areas, play-
ground, pool, community cen-
ter

Walnut Community Center
NE
3808 Cecile Ave.
Picnic area, swimming pool,
community center

West Flamingo Park
SW
6255 W. Flamingo
Ball fields, picnic areas, play-
ground, volleyball, skateboard-
ing, walking-jogging trail,
active adult center

Whitney Park & Community
Center
SE
5700 Missouri
Playground, picnic areas, bas-
ketball, restrooms, community
garden, tennis

**Winchester Park &
Community Center**
SE
3130 S. McLeod
*Ball fields, picnic areas, play-
ground, tennis, basketball,
community garden, spray pool,
theater, gallery, performance
area, exercise course, walking
path*

**Winterwood Park/Wengert
School Park**
SE
*Ball field, picnic areas, play-
ground, tennis, restrooms,
walking and jogging path, fitness apparatus*

Source: Las Vegas Perspective Survey, 2000.

Appendix

Las Vegas Golf Courses

Angel Park Golf Club

Two Arnold Palmer-designed courses (Mountain and Palm) highlight Angel Park, dubbed the world's most complete golf experience. Cloud Nine, a lighted par 3 with holes with similar shot values to some of golf's most famous par 3 holes, the world-famous all-grass putting course, a lighted range and full-service clubhouse facilities are also available. Private, Group, Junior Lessons and Deluxe Golf Schools available on site at Resort Golf Academies. Professionally managed by OB Sports. 100 South Rampart Blvd., Las Vegas, NV 89128 (702) 254-4653, (888) 851-4114, www.angelpark.com.

Badlands Golf Club

Hall-of-Famer Johnny Miller and two-time Las Vegas Senior Classic winner Chi Chi Rodriguez teamed to design 27 holes of dynamic golf at the Badlands, once named a favorite in a *Las Vegas Review-Journal* newspaper poll. The original 18, the Desperado and Diablo nines, meander through rugged desert canyons and offer shot values not found anywhere else. Accuracy and ball position are vital. The Outlaw nine is home to wide fairways and player-friendly golf. Clubhouse, practice and banquet facilities available. Ken Venturi Golf School and American Golf's Nike Golf Learning Center on site. 9119 Alta Dr., Las Vegas, NV 89128; (702) 382-4653, (800) 468-7918, www.americangolf.com.

Bali Hai Golf Course

Situated right on the Las Vegas Strip, this tropical-themed golf course is reminiscent of courses in the South Pacific. The course is highlighted by an island green, numerous large water features, and thick stands of towering palms, tropical plants and flowers. Transition and out-of-play areas are accented with beach sand and volcanic rock outcroppings to further add to the authentic island atmosphere. Caddies available, special events area for groups and tournaments. The clubhouse also features Cili, the newest dining experience on the strip by the world famous Chef Wolfgang Puck. Cili is open for lunch and dinner, Monday through Saturday. For reservations, 856-1000. 5160 Las Vegas Blvd. South,

Las Vegas, NV 89119; (702) 450-8000 or (888) 397-2499, www.waltersgolf.com.

Black Mountain Golf & Country Club

One of the oldest courses in the area, Black Mountain's 18 holes meander through neighborhoods in Henderson, a suburb of Las Vegas. The Black Mountain range overlooks the semi-private course that is home to wide fairways, smallish greens and many trees. A new clubhouse and driving range are available. PGA Tour players Craig Barlow and Edward Fryatt grew up playing Black Mountain. 500 Greenway Rd., Henderson, NV 89015; (702) 565-7933, www.golfblackmountain.com.

Callaway Golf Center

113-tee station driving range. Par 3 golf course, performance center. 6730 Las Vegas Blvd., Las Vegas, NV 89119; (702) 896-4100, www.callawaygolfcenter.com.

Craig Ranch Golf Course

Walking is allowed at Craig Ranch, a short course set in a rural setting and shadowed by hundreds of trees. A mostly locals layout, the facility is home to a driving range and small pro shop. Wide open holes make Craig Ranch a perfect place for beginning players. 628 W. Craig Rd., North Las Vegas, NV 89030; (702) 642-9700.

Desert Inn Golf Club

This beautiful, tradition-rich 18-hole championship golf course, the only championship course on the Las Vegas Strip that has hosted the PGA Tour, the LPGA Tour, the Senior PGA Tour and the Las Vegas Intercollegiate, is now closed. Look for a new course to be built on this site.

Desert Pines Golf Course

Located just 15 minutes from the Strip and five minutes from downtown, this traditional course showcases more than 4,000 towering pines, natural Carolina landscaping and white sand bunkers. Desert Pines offers a "country club for a day experience" and was nominated as the best new upscale golf course by *Golf Digest* and was voted "Best course in Las Vegas" by readers of the *Las Vegas Review-Journal.* On-site is the Desert Pines Golf Center. 3415 E. Bonanza Rd., Las Vegas, NV 89101; (702) 450-8000, (888) 397-2499, www.waltersgolf.com.

Desert Rose Golf Course

Las Vegas locals' best kept secret! Designed by Joe Lee and Dick Wilson, Desert Rose offers a forgiving layout that's challenging for all levels of play. Full practice facility, restaurant and snack bar available. Affordably priced and conveniently located just 7.5 miles east of the Las Vegas strip or downtown. So avoid the traffic and enjoy the "Best Value" in Las Vegas. Desert Rose is a facility of Clark County. 5483

Club House Dr., Las Vegas, NV 89122; (702) 431-4653.

Desert Willow Golf Club

Designed by PGA Tour Hall-of-Famer Billy Casper and architect Greg Nash, the executive-length Desert Willow is home to six par 4s and 12 par 3s. Tucked into the Black Mountain range, the course provides tremendous views of the valley. Finely manicured fairways and greens, and lakes with fountains. Desert Willow is the perfect place for a quick round, as the average 18 holes takes a little over three hours to play. 2020 W. Horizon Ridge Pkwy., Henderson, NV 89012; (702) 263-4653, www.desertwillowlasvegas.com.

Eagle Crest Golf Club

Eagle Crest is one of five Billy Casper/Greg Nash designs in the Las Vegas Valley. The executive-length layout is home to six par 4s and 12 par 3s and is located in the master-planned Sun City Summerlin retirement community. Plenty of challenge is available and Eagle Crest is a good place to go for a quick 18. 2203 Thomas Ryan Blvd., Las Vegas, NV 89134; (702) 240-1320, www.delwebb.com.

Highland Falls Golf Club

Billy Casper won 51 times on the PGA Tour, and has teamed five times with Greg Nash to design courses in the Las Vegas area. Highland Falls is highlighted by quick greens, expansive views of the Las Vegas valley and holes played over water features and around sporadic desert canyons. The course is semi-private and is played with Red Rock Canyon providing a beautiful backdrop. 10201 Sun City Blvd., Las Vegas, NV 89134; (702) 254-7010.

Las Vegas Golf Club

The oldest course in Las Vegas is one of the busiest layouts in the country. The course is a local favorite and recently underwent $4 million worth of renovations. Wide, tree-lined fairways, a lighted driving range and a new clubhouse highlight the city-owned facility. Monte Money, a Las Vegas legend, owns the course record of 58. 4300 W. Washington Ave., Las Vegas, NV 89107; (702) 646-3003, www.americangolf.com.

Las Vegas National Golf Club

Las Vegas National is a traditional course located minutes from the Las Vegas Strip. The course has played host to both the LPGA and PGA Tour over the years and was one of three in the Las Vegas Invitational rotation when Tiger Woods won his first PGA Tour event in 1996. Five tough par 3s and several dog-legged holes accent the layout, which is operated by American Golf Corporation. Clubhouse, pro shop, lighted driving range and banquet facilities are available. 1911 E. Desert Inn Rd., Las Vegas, NV 89109; (702) 382-4653, (800) 468-7918, www.americangolf.com.

Las Vegas Paiute Resort Sun Mountain & Snow Mountain Courses

Two Pete Dye-designed (Snow and Sun Mountain) courses highlight the Las Vegas Paiute Resort. Symbolic Dye railroad ties, distinct bunkering and visually demanding holes highlight the player-friendly layouts. Native flowering, lakes and expansive views of the desert terrain accent the round. The resort houses a complete practice area and a 50,000-square-foot clubhouse. 10325 Nu-Wav Kaiv Blvd., Las Vegas, NV 89124; (702) 658-1400, (888) 921-2833, www.lvpaiutegolf.com.

Legacy Golf Club

Legacy is home to 18 holes of championship golf by Arthur Hills, featuring numerous bunkers, rolling mounds, large greens and multiple level fairways. Ranked as one of the "top ten courses to play in Nevada" by *Golf Digest*, the Legacy Golf Club plays host annually to the local U.S. Open Qualifier and the AJGA. The links design provides a complete golf experience for the player of any ability level. Full-service restaurant/banquet facilities and snack bar, a 30-station driving range, on-course beverage service and PGA instruction round out the Legacy's amenities. Private, group, junior lessons and deluxe golf schools available on site at Resort Golf Academies. 130 Par Excellence Dr., Henderson, NV; (702) 897-2187, (888) 446-5358, www.thelega-cygc.com.

Los Prados Golf Course

This executive-length layout stretches throughout the Los Prados housing community. Many of the par 3s average 300 yards. Clubhouse facilities with tennis courts and banquet rooms are available at this semi-private course. 5150 Los Prados Cir., Las Vegas, NV 89130; (702) 645-5696.

North Las Vegas Golf Course

This North Las Vegas par 3 course is lighted and provides a good opportunity for beginners to learn the game of golf. 324 E. Brooks Ave., North Las Vegas, NV 89030; (702) 633-1833.

Painted Desert Golf Club

Painted Desert was the first desert course in the Las Vegas area, and features emerald green fairways and greens, and holes shaped by desert waste areas with some forced carries. Water features, cacti and many bunkers decorate the course. Driving range, clubhouse with pro shop, and Nike Golf Learning Center, lessons are available at this property. 5555 Painted Mirage, Las Vegas, NV 89149; (702) 645-2570, (800) 468-7918, www.americangolf.com.

Palm Valley Golf Club

Billy Casper and Greg Nash designed the Palm Valley course, and it is home to typical Casper/Nash beauty and intrigue. Flowers, lakes and holes that flow throughout the Sun City

Summerlin neighborhoods provide challenge for all players. Sun City courses are highlighted by greens that break toward the valley and elevated holes offering views of Las Vegas. 9201 Del Webb Blvd., Las Vegas, NV 89134; (702) 363-4373, www.suncitygolf.com.

Reflection Bay Golf Club

The second Jack Nicklaus-designed course at the exclusive, $4 billion Lake Las Vegas Resort; Reflection Bay is open to the public. Annually, the course plays host to the nationally televised Wendy's Three-Tour Challenge. The championship master-piece has five holes that play directly along 1.5 miles of shoreline of the 32-acre Lake Las Vegas. Additional features are spectacular views of sur-rounding mountains, waterfalls, and play around natural canyons. 75 MonteLago Blvd., Henderson, NV 89011; (702) 740-4653, (877) 698-4653, www.lakelasvegas.com.

Revere at Anthem

Designed by PGA legend Billy Casper and architect Greg Nash, The Revere Golf Club at Anthem is located at Del Webb's new Anthem Community, and just 15 minutes from the famed Las Vegas Strip. Built in a desert canyon, the lush 7,143-yard, par 72 course features countless natural elevation changes and beautiful views of the Las Vegas skyline. Recently, the course was named one of the "Top New Courses You Can Play" by *Golf Magazine*. 2600

Hampton, Henderson, NV 89052; (702) 259-4653, (877) 278-8373, www.revereatanthem.com.

Rhodes Ranch Golf Club

Rhodes Ranch is a Ted Robinson design that is home to tough, intriguing par 3s, paralleling fairways and numerous water features. Robinson says the par 3s are the best combination he's ever designed, highlighted by the third hole that plays over water to a green backdropped by palm trees. Hundreds of additional palm trees accent the course, tucked within the shadows of the Spanish Mountain range. Rhodes Ranch is a player-friendly course. 20 Rhodes Ranch Pkwy., Las Vegas, NV 89113; (702) 740-4114, (888) 311-8337, www.rhodesranch.com.

Rio Secco Golf Club

Rio Secco, a Rees Jones design, is the crown jewel of the Rio All-Suite Casino Resort. Played throughout the southeast Las Vegas desert, Rio Secco exquisitely combines six plateau holes, six canyon holes and six desert holes. A new clubhouse is now open at the facility, where Butch Harmon, Tiger Woods' teacher, heads the Butch Harmon School of Golf. Golf packages through the Rio Suite Hotel and Casino are available. Par 72. 2851 Grand Hills Dr., Henderson, NV 89012; (702) 889-2400, (888) 867-3226, www.playrio.com.

Royal Links Golf Club

Voted by *Golf Magazine* as one of the "Top Ten New

Courses to Play." Just 15 minutes from the Strip and a must-play for golfers who appreciate the great lore and tradition of the game, Royal Links is a tribute to the game's history and the closest you'll get to a British Open experience on this side of the Pond. Each hole at Royal Links is designed after a great hole from courses played during the British Open. Holes featured include Royal Troon's Postage Stamp and St. Andrews' Road Hole. From exceptional customer service to the forecaddies and caddies, Royal Links offers a truly special golfing experience. A Walters Golf Property. Par 72, four sets of tees. Yardages range from 5,142-7,029. 5995 E. Vegas Valley Rd., Las Vegas, NV 89122; (702) 450-8000, (800) 397-2499, www.waltersgolf.com.

Shadow Creek Golf Club

Shadow Creek, a Tom Fazio and Steve Wynn design, is one of the best golf courses in the world and is annually ranked as such by national golf publications. Only guests of MGM/Mirage can play the layout. Caddies, first-class service, wildlife, lakes, and more highlight a round at Shadow Creek. 3 Shadow Creek Dr, North Las Vegas, NV 89031; (702) 791-7161, (888) 778-3387, www.mirageresorts.com.

Siena Golf Club

The elevated characteristic of the terrain provides panoramic mountain and city views. The Schmidt-Curley designed course also features Lake Siena, a quarter-mile long lake with cascading waterfalls on the first hole. The Siena Golf Club offers a full-service golf shop, multi-tiered practice facility and The Grille at Siena with a patio dining room overlooking the 18th fairway. Par 72 Yards 6816 (71.5/129). 10575 Siena Monte Ave., Las Vegas, NV 89135; (702) 341-9200, (888) 689-6469, www.sienagolfclub.com.

Silverstone Golf Club

This Robert Cupp course features 27 holes and is the most recent addition to the Vegas Valley. A special 28th hole can decide bets. (702) 562-3770, (877) 888-2127, www.silverstonegolf.com.

Sunrise Vista Golf Club

Sunrise Vista is an outstanding 36-hole golf facility located on Nellis AFB. Nellis AFB is the home of the world-famous Thunderbirds squadron. Golfers might be treated to some classic practice air maneuvers while enjoying a round of golf. Three of the four nines are named after fighter jets. The fourth nine is named after the Thunderbirds squadron. An 18-acre driving range sports an army tank as one of the range targets. While this facility is primarily for military personnel and their guests, civilians are welcome to call the pro shop and to come out and play a first class military facility. 2841 Kinley Dr., Las Vegas, NV 89191; (702) 652-2602, wwwmil.nellis.af.mil/golf.

TPC at the Canyons

The Tournament Players Club at The Canyons creatively combines personal service and unique aesthetic qualities. The course, designed by PGA Tour Design Services with Raymond Floyd as player consultant, can be described as desert elegance. TPC at the Canyons, cohost of the Invensys Classic at Las Vegas, features a multitude of trees, elevation changes and steep ravines. Reservations are taken up to 180 days in advance. Golf packages are available through JW Marriott. Par 71. 9851 Canyon Run Dr., Las Vegas, NV 89144; (702) 256-2000, www.tpc.com.

Wildhorse Golf Club

Wildhorse is home to hundreds of trees, many shimmering lakes and greens guarded by bunkers. The American Golf Corporation property hosted the PGA Tour in the 1960s when it was named Paradise Valley Country Club. The finishing 18th hole is highlighted by five separate water features. The clubhouse overlooks the course with a patio available for outside seating. Banquet facilities are available. Par 72. 2100 Warm Springs Rd., Henderson, NV 89014; (702) 382-4653, (888) 468-7918, www.americangolf.com.

Anthem Country Club

"From the impressive setting to the sweeping elevation changes, this is a course that has been crafted to stand apart from the crowd," Senior PGA Tour Player of the Year and player consultant Hale Irwin says about Keith Foster's course design. Built at an elevation of 3,000 feet, the course weaves majestically through the natural desert terrain of the Southern Nevada desert with many holes played through canyons and highlighted by waterfalls and native landscaping. For a limited time, outside play is being accepted. The course is located in the Anthem master-planned community. Par 72. One Clubside Drive, Henderson, NV 89054; (702) 614-5050, www.delwebb.com.

Canyon Gate Country Club

Canyon Gate is a lush Ted Robinson design located in the Canyon Gate community of homes. The course is home to Robinson-trademarked rolling hills and several water hazards, including a beautiful waterfall adjacent to the 18th green. Managed by Club Corporation of America, the club offers limited reciprocal play. Memberships are still available. 2001 Canyon Gate Dr., Las Vegas, NV 89117; (702) 363-0303.

Las Vegas Country Club

The private layout is adjacent to the Las Vegas Hilton Hotel and is a host site for the Las Vegas Invitational. Majestic trees, long, tough par 4s and well-bunkered holes highlight the course where Senior PGA Tour player Larry Laorretti once served as a golf professional. 3000 Joe W. Brown Dr., Las Vegas, NV 89109; (702) 734-1122.

Red Rock Country Club

Two private, world-class Arnold Palmer designed championship golf courses highlight this exclusive community. The first 18 holes are open. Several membership options are available for both Red Rock residents and non-Red Rock residents. Home prices start from the low $300,000s to more than one million. 2250 Red Springs, Las Vegas, NV 89135; (702) 360-5959, (800) 856-6885, www.redrockcountryclub.com.

SouthShore Golf Club at Lake Las Vegas Resort

SouthShore was Jack Nicklaus' first design in Nevada, and combines such distinct Nicklaus features as bunker-guarded small greens and holes that place a premium on long-iron play. The course is located in the multi-billion-dollar Lake Las Vegas Resort, an exclusive community home to a 320-acre private lake, a members-only club, and other amenities. 29 Grand Mediterranean Dr., Henderson, NV 89011; (702) 558-0022, (800) 427-6682, www.lake-lasvegas.com.

Southern Highlands Golf Club

The 220-acre golf course is one of only three worldwide codesigned by Robert Trent Jones, Sr. and Robert Trent Jones, Jr. The challenging 7,381 yard, par 72 course offers sweeping elevation changes over rolling landscaped terrain. Breathtaking views of the nearby mountains and the Las Vegas skyline provide a beautiful backdrop for play. One Robert Trent Jones Lane, Las Vegas, NV 89141; (702) 263-1000, www.southernhighlandsgolfclub.com.

Spanish Trail Country Club

Spanish Trail is a 27-hole facility designed by Robert Trent Jones Jr. that has played host to PGA Tour and college golf tournaments. Limited reciprocal arrangements are available. 5050 Spanish Trail Lane, Las Vegas, NV 89113; (702) 364-0357, www.spanishtrailcc.com.

Stallion Mountain Country Club

Stallion Mountain is located just 15 minutes from the Strip. The gated, 54-hole private facility is accessible to guests staying at one of the Las Vegas hotels that have a corporate membership. Reciprocal play available to out-of-town members of private golf clubs. The Man O' War Course has hosted the Las Vegas Invitational; the Citation Course hosted the Frank Sinatra Celebrity Golf Classic and in its debut, the Secretariat Course was recognized as one of the top 10 new courses. Two distinctly separate clubhouses accommodate members and guests, and the John Jacobs Golf School is on-site. A Walters Golf property. 5500 E. Flamingo Rd., Las Vegas, NV 89122; (702) 450-8000, (888) 397-2499, www.waltersgolf.com.

TPC at Summerlin

Fuzzy Zoeller, winner of the first Las Vegas Invitational, was the player consultant on this PGA Tour Design Services course, a part of the Tournament Players Club network of courses. The facility annually hosts the PGA Tour, and was the site of Tiger Woods' first PGA Tour victory. 1700 Village Center Cir., Las Vegas, NV 89134; (702) 256-0222, www.playatpc.com.

Boulder City Golf Course

Located in Boulder City, home of Hoover Dam, this course is shadowed by hundreds of large trees and is home to large greens, wide open fairways and two lakes. Reachable par 5s, tricky par 3s and straight-forward par 4s allow golfers of all abilities to enjoy the layout. A quaint clubhouse, driving range and lessons are available, and walking is allowed. Par 72. 1 Clubhouse Dr., Boulder City, NV 89005; (702) 293-9236.

Emerald River Golf Course

Located just minutes from Laughlin's glittering hotels and casinos, Emerald River offers a pic-turesque and challenging 18 holes of champi-onship-caliber golf through the desert canyons overlooking the Colorado River. The holes are demanding but offer golfers a truly unique experi-ence. The course has been rated number one in dif-ficulty by the Nevada Golf Association. Golf packages are available with several Laughlin hotels. Par 72. 1155 W. Casino Dr., Laughlin, NV 89028; (702) 298-4653, www.americangolf.com.

Mojave Resort Golf Club

Mojave Resort Golf Club is a championship resort course with wide, friendly fairways and four sets of tees, allowing golfers to choose their own challenge. A terrain that combines native vegetation with wind-shaped sand dunes provided the setting for Landmark Golf Company, in conjunction with CNC Entertainment Nevada, Inc., to develop this layout. Emerald fairways laid upon delicate desert sand dunes accent the course. Voted best course in tri-state area. Par 72. 9905 Aha Macav Pkwy., Laughlin, NV 89029; (702) 535-4653, www.mojaveresort.com.

CasaBlanca Golf Club

The Cal Olsen-designed CasaBlanca Golf Club lies etched into the wetlands of the Mesquite Valley. This beautiful course winds in and out of the Virgin River basin offering a new experience on every tee. Five sets of tees allow golfers of all skill levels a fair chance on this course which annually hosts the Nevada Open. Golf Packages are available with the CasaBlanca Hotel/Casino that is home to a world-class spa. CasaBlanca Golf Club is also home to Shot Makers Golf School. Par 72. 1100 Hafen Lane, Mesquite, NV 89027; (702) 346-7529, (888) 711-4653, www.casablancaresort.com.

Wolf Creek Golf Resort

Created around natural desert arroyos, Wolf Creek offers an intimidating yet unusually picturesque and player-friendly design. With five sets of tees and generous landing areas, each tee shot places a premium on accuracy, while the contoured bent grass greens offer several challenging pin placements. Par 72. Mesquite, NV 89027; (866) 252-4653, www.PlaytheWolf.com.

Palms Golf Club

The Palms championship course comprises lakes, sand traps and more than 200 palm trees and is a challenge for all levels of player. The layout is two courses in one as the front nine offers extended fairways and plenty of water features, while the back nine provides a mountainous style of golf where shot placement is key. The 15th hole has a breathtaking view and a vertical drop of 115 feet from the tee to the fairway. Par 72. 711 Palms Blvd., Mesquite, NV 89024; (702) 346-5232, (800) 621-0187, www.oasisresort.com.

Oasis Golf Club

There are 27 holes of golf at the Oasis Golf Club. The Arnold Palmer-designed Oasis Golf Course was recognized as one of the top five best new golf courses in North America and is rated among the top 10 you can play by *Golf Digest*. The Oasis is home to five sets of tees and features scenic desert panoramas.

Rugged canyon fairways and contoured greens make this one of Palmer's most distinctive designs. The Vistas Nine is home to rugged canyon fairways, contoured greens and spectacular desert panoramas. 851 Oasis Blvd., Mesquite, NV 89024; (702) 346-5232, (888) 367-3386, www.the oasisgolfclub.com.

Primm Valley Golf Club

Two Tom Fazio-designed courses (the Lakes and Desert) offer two different, distinct golf course designs. The Lakes is a traditional course home to wide fairways, lush landscape and several water features including waterfalls. The Desert course is a player-friendly desert-styled course home to cacti, desert-lined fairways and desert waste areas. Golf packages are available through the Primm Valley Resort and the MGM Grand Hotel. 31900 Las Vegas Blvd. South, Primm, NV 89019; (702) 679-5510, (800) 386-7867, www.primmvalleyresorts.com.

Willow Creek

Plain and simple, it's worth the 60-mile drive to Pahrump just for the chance to play this course. The par 72 championship layout is a good challenge for all players, and the price is right. (755) 727-4653.

This information was provided courtesy of the Las Vegas Review-Journal. *An updated version of this list can be found on the web at lvrj.com.*

Appendix

Professional and Occupational Licensing Boards

For those professionals moving to Las Vegas, it may be helpful to have the contact information for the professional board which applies to your occupation. They are listed below.

Nevada State Board of Accountancy
200 South Virginia Street, Suite 670
Reno, Nevada 89501-2408
Telephone: (775) 786-2408
Fax: (775) 786-0234

State Board of Architecture, Interior Design and Residential Design
2080 East Flamingo Rd., Suite 225

Las Vegas, NV 89119-5179
Telephone: (702) 486-7300
Fax: (702) 486-7304

Board of Examiners for Audiology and Speech
Pathology
P.O. Box 70550
Reno, NV 89570-0550
Telephone: (775) 857-3500
Fax: (775) 857-2121

State Barbers' Health and Sanitation Board
4710 East Flamingo Rd.
Las Vegas, NV 89121-4709
Telephone: (702) 456-6700

Chiropractic Physicians' Board of Nevada
4600 Kietzke Lane, Bldg. M, Suite 245
Reno, NV 89502-5000
Telephone: (775) 688-1921
Fax: (775) 688-1920

State Contractors' Board

> Las Vegas Office:
> 4220 S. Maryland Pkwy., Suite D-800
> Las Vegas, NV 89119-7533
> Telephone: (702) 486-1100
> Fax: (702) 486-1190

> Reno Office:
> 9670 Gateway Drive, Suite 100
> Reno, NV 89511

Telephone: (775) 688-1141
Fax: (775) 688-1271

State Board of Cosmetology
1785 East Sahara Ave., Suite 255
Las Vegas, NV 89104-3716
Telephone: (702) 486-6542
Fax: (702) 369-8064

Certified Court Reporters' Board of Nevada
P.O. Box 237
Las Vegas, NV 89125-0237
Telephone: (702) 384-1663

Board of Dental Examiners of Nevada
2225 Renaissance Drive, Suite E
Las Vegas, NV 89119-6164
Telephone: (702) 486-7044

State Board of Professional Engineers and Land
Surveyors
1755 East Plumb Lane, Suite 135
Reno, NV 89502-3632
Telephone: (775) 688-1231
Fax: (775) 688-2991

State Board of Funeral Directors, Embalmers and
Operators of Cemeteries and Crematories
4894 Lone Mountain Rd., Suite 186
Las Vegas, NV 89130-2239
Telephone: (702) 646-6860
Fax: (702) 648-5858

Board of Hearing Aid Specialists
3172 N. Rainbow Blvd., Suite 141
Las Vegas, NV 89108-4534
Telephone: (702) 571-9000

Board of Homeopathic Medical Examiners
P.O. Box 34329
Las Vegas, NV 89133-4329
Telephone: (702) 258-5487
Fax: (702) 258-5487

Board of Landscape Architecture
P.O. Box 51780
Sparks, NV 89435-1780
Telephone/Fax: (775) 359-8110

Board of Examiners for Marriage and Family
Therapists
P.O. Box 72758
Las Vegas, NV 89170-2758
Telephone: (702) 486-7388

Board of Medical Examiners
P.O. Box 7238
Reno, NV 89502-2162
Telephone: (775) 688-2559

State Board of Nursing
4330 South Valley View, Suite 106
Las Vegas, NV 89103-4126
Telephone: (702) 486-5800
Fax: (702) 486-5803

Board of Occupational Therapy
P.O. Box 70220
Reno, NV 89570-0220
Telephone: (775) 857-1700
Fax: (775) 857-2121

Board of Dispensing Opticians
P.O. Box 70503
Reno, NV 89570-0503
Telephone: (775) 345-1444
Fax: (775) 853-1421

Nevada State Board of Optometry
P.O. Box 1824
Carson City, NV 89702-1824
Telephone: (775) 883-8367
Fax: (775) 883-1938

State Board of Oriental Medicine
201 Sarah Drive
Carson City, NV 89706-0575
Telephone: (702) 486-4279

State Board of Osteopathic Medicine
2950 East Flamingo Rd., Suite E-3
Las Vegas, NV 89121-5208
Telephone: (702) 732-2147
Fax: (702) 732-2079

State Board of Pharmacy
1201 Terminal Way, Suite 212
Reno, NV 89502-3257

Telephone: (775) 322-0691
Fax: (775) 322-0895

State Board of Physical Therapy Examiners
P.O. Box 81467
Las Vegas, NV 89180-1467
Telephone: (702) 876-5535
Fax: (702) 876-2097

State Board of Podiatry
2413 South Eastern Ave., Suite 142
Las Vegas, NV 89104-4102
Telephone: (702) 733-7617

Board of Psychological Examiners
P.O. Box 2286
Reno, NV 89505-2286
Telephone: (775) 688-1268

Board of Examiners for Social Workers
4600 Kietzke Ln., Building C, Suite 121
Reno, NV 89502-5035
Telephone: (775) 688-2555
Fax: (775) 688-2557

Nevada State Board of Veterinary
Medical Examiners
4600 Kietzke Ln., Building O, Suite 265
Reno, NV 89502-5046
Telephone: (775) 688-1788
Fax: (775) 688-1808

Appendix

Las Vegas Climate

Yes, Las Vegas is a desert town, but that doesn't mean it's always hot. In fact, desert climate means great extremes in temperature. The table on the following page shows climate data for the months of the year.

Feature	Year	Jan	Feb	Mar	Apr	May	Jun	Jul	Aug	Sep	Oct	Nov	Dec
High Temperature (avg.)*	80	56	62	69	78	88	99	104	102	94	81	66	57
Low Temperature (avg.) *	53	33	38	43	51	60	69	76	74	66	54	41	34
Precipitation (average) (inches)	4	0.5	0.4	0.4	0.2	0.2	0.1	0.4	0.5	0.3	0.2	0.4	0.3
Snow (average) (inches)	1	1	0	0	0	0	0	0	0	0	0	0	0
Humidity (percent relative)	20	32	25	20	15	13	10	14	16	16	18	26	31

*All temperatures reported in degrees Fahrenheit.

Appendix

Annual Events

January

Chinese New Year
Asian-Pacific Cultural Center
4215 Spring Mountain Rd.
(702) 221-8448

In Las Vegas' own "Chinatown," Chinese New Year is celebrated with various entertainers, cultural exhibits, even a mahjong tournament. Many oriental restaurants are housed here, so good food is a large feature of this event. Call the center for specifics as this event varies by date.

February

Las Vegas Marathon
S.R. 604 to Las Vegas
(702) 876-3870

This annual race begins in the small town of Sloan, Nevada and ends at Sunset Park near McCarran Airport. Smaller races—half marathons and relays—are available for the less-competitive.

March

Mountain West Conference Basketball Tournament
Thomas & Mack Center, UNLV
(702) 895-3900

The west's top basketball teams compete in this tournament, which brings lively crowds and some great games our way. The tournament lasts six days and includes men's and women's teams.

Busch Grand National Race
7000 Las Vegas Blvd. North
(800) 644-4444

The Las Vegas Motor Speedway offers many events each year, but this is a big NASCAR race which brings in tens of thousands of visitors to our area. Also see the 400 Winston Cup Race with stock cars. Get your tickets early as they are popular.

Corporate Challenge
749 Veterans Memorial Drive
(702) 229-6706

From March to April, more than 100 teams

based on the size of their employers compete in various sports including volleyball, bowling, golf, field events, etc. Teams win gold, silver and bronze medals at closing ceremonies as well as trophies. This is a popular event, and employers pick up the tab for the costs involved.

St. Patrick's Day Parade
Fremont Street
(702) 678-5600

This parade is the best attended of the local parades. Come see most of our government representatives and various businesses and civic organizations represented. The weather is usually perfect this time of year and it makes for a pleasant few hours.

Big League Weekend
Cashman Field
850 Las Vegas Blvd. North
(702) 386-7200

It's not that we don't appreciate the Las Vegas 51s, our local triple-A baseball team. But it's hard to find a spare ticket when several professional baseball teams come into town to play preseason games.

April

Clark County Fair
Fairgrounds, Logandale
(702) 398-3249

Just 45 minutes north of Las Vegas (take I-15), this fair is much like you remember from your childhood. Juried exhibits, livestock and craft com-petitions, lots of good food, and many carnival rides make for a fun family experience.

World Series of Poker
Binion's Horseshoe
128 Fremont Street
(702) 382-1600

Some of the best poker players in the world arrive in town for this high-stakes tournament. This event is free to the public.

Earth Fair
Sunset Park
2601 E. Sunset Rd.
(702) 455-8289

Free trees, crafts, learning about how to protect our planet—these are a few of the features of this fun gathering. Make it a day and bring a picnic or buy lunch at the food booths.

May

Art in the Park
Hills Park
9099 Hillpointe Rd.
(702) 229-6511

This free show, well worth attending, offers a large number of artisans displaying their wares. From the lowest-price trinket to a major art piece, you will find it here. Usually held during the first weekend in May, it is open 10 AM to 6 PM Saturday and Sunday.

Jazz in the Park
Clark County Government Center
500 Grand Central Parkway
(702) 455-8242

In May and June, several jazz concerts are held in the outdoor amphitheater. Free admission and a casual atmosphere make this great for families. Bring a picnic dinner and enjoy the cool weather. Blankets or low chairs are helpful as this is a grass area.

July

Independence Day
Desert Breeze Park
8425 Spring Mountain Rd.
(702) 455-8206

Come very early (some arrive mid-afternoon) to stake out a good place for your family to enjoy the festivities at Desert Breeze Park. Entertainment, contests, and food vendors add to the fun, but the big event is the spectacular fireworks display after dark. Picnics are welcome.

Boulder City Damboree
Central Park, Boulder City
(702) 293-9256

This all-day event features a community breakfast, a concert, a parade, and a fireworks display at night.

August

Helldorado Days
Thomas & Mack Center, UNLV
(702) 870-1221

One of Las Vegas' longest-running events, the Helldorado offers four days of family fun. Rodeos, exhibits, competitions, a dancing hall and carnival rides offer something for almost anyone.

September

Chautauqua Festival
Bicentennial Park, Boulder City
(702) 294-6224

Have a conversation with Mark Twain or listen to Abraham Lincoln tell his story. These figures and many others grace us each year. Bring a picnic dinner and watch the show, or join the group for the opening night dinner and reception. All prices are low.

Shakespeare in the Park
Foxridge Park, Warm Springs and Valle Verde, Henderson
(702) 458-8855

Bring a blanket and a picnic dinner for some wonderfully entertaining plays in a beautiful park. Strolling entertainers keep you occupied before the show begins. Friday and Saturday shows begin at 7; Sunday's show starts at 6 PM.

October

Jaycee State Fair
Cashman Field, 350 Las Vegas Blvd. North
(702) 457-3247

This fair runs for six days and features many exhibits, carnival rides, food booths and various entertainment.

Art in the Park
Bicentennial Park, Boulder City
(702) 294-1611

This is the big one. The largest art fair in the area offers more than 300 exhibitors with wildly varied media. Plan to spend most of the day just to get a look at all the booths. Because this show is so popular, lines tend to get long at the food booths. With plenty of parks available in Boulder City, it's wise to pack a picnic lunch to escape the crowd. Take the time to stroll through downtown Boulder City with its quaint shops and old-time feel.

November

Western Heritage Festival
Community College of Southern Nevada
3200 E. Cheyenne Ave., North Las Vegas
(702) 658-4679

Come hear cowboy poetry, music, and visit the various vendors and craft booths. Often you will see a display of hot air balloons.

December

National Finals Rodeo
Thomas & Mack Center, UNLV
(702) 260-8605

For ten days, Las Vegas becomes a cowboy town. Every country-western singer appears at the Strip hotels to entertain those who come to town for this event. This is a full rodeo with big prize money. You can purchase tickets by the day or for the whole event.

Parade of Lights
Lake Mead Marina
322 Lakeshore Rd., Boulder City
(702) 457-2797

This magical event features boats lit up for the holidays. If you dress warmly it proves a very pleasant way to kick off the holiday season.

New Year's Eve

Las Vegas Strip and Fremont Street

Just about anywhere you stand on Las Vegas Boulevard, you'll see a fabulous fireworks display at midnight. Fireworks are launched from several major Strip resorts, and for a few minutes, it seems like the whole world is covered with brilliant color. The Strip becomes very crowded, and the crowds can be rowdy.

Appendix

Recreation Centers

Valley View Recreation Center
500 Harris Street
(702) 565-2121

The center features a 40,000 square feet space, gymnasium, 3 racquetball/volleyball courts, 6 meeting/classrooms, multi-fitness room, multi-use room, game room, and vending area. The first full-service recreation center to open in the City of Henderson, the Lorna J. Kesterson Valley View Recreation Center services the Valley View area. Located adjacent to Morrell Park. This center services all ages in all areas of interest, however is best known as being the home for the City's own

Henderson Civic Symphony. M-F 8 AM to 9 PM, Sat 9 AM to 5 PM, and Sun 1 PM to 5 PM.

Chuck Minker Sports Complex
(Next to Rivera Park)
275 N. Mojave Rd.
(702) 229-6563

The sports complex features a gymnasium, 8 racquetball courts, cardiovascular equipment, sauna & jacuzzi, 2 weight rooms, free & machine weights, multipurpose room, video games, and locker rooms. Gym and multipurpose room for rent. M-F, 7 AM to 9:30 PM, Sat, 9 AM to 5 PM, and Sun, 10 AM to 4 PM.

Doolittle Community Center
(Next to Doolittle Park)
1950 N "J" St
(702) 229-6374
Ingrid Williams - Center Coordinator

The recreational center features fitness room, full basketball court, game room, gymnasium, 3 meeting rooms, conference room, and kitchen facilities. M-F, 9 AM to 4 PM and Sat, 9 AM to 4 PM.

HENDERSON

Black Mountain Recreation Center and Aquatic Complex
599 Greenway Road
(702) 565-2880

The Black Mountain Recreation Center/ Aquatic Complex is the first to sport a zero-depth entry aquatic complex which features a three loop slide, interactive water apparatus and raindrop waterfall. The complex features 41,000 square feet, gymnasium, 3 racquetball/volleyball courts, 6 meeting/classrooms, multi-fitness room, multi-use room, game room, vending area, and beach-entry pool. M-F 8 AM to 9 PM, Sat 9 AM to 5 PM, and Sun 1PM to 5PM.

Silver Springs Recreation Center
1951 Silver Springs Parkway
(702) 435-3814

Serving the entire Green Valley area of Henderson. Whether it be tots to seniors, or teens to adults, you will find it at this center which—like any of the city's full-service recreation centers—is open seven days a week. Throughout the summer months, enjoy the Silver Springs Outdoor Swimming Pool as well. Benefits for life. Features 36,000 square feet of space, gymnasium, 3 racquetball/volleyball courts, 6 meeting/classrooms, multi-fitness room, multi-use room, game room, vending area, and clubhouse. M–F 8 AM to 9 PM, Sat 9 AM to 5 PM, and Sun 1 PM to 5 PM.

Whitney Ranch Recreation Center and Aquatic Complex
1575 Galleria Drive
(702) 450-5885

The center features 41,000 square feet of space, gymnasium, 3 racquetball/walleyball courts, 2 meeting rooms/ 3 classrooms, dance & aerobics room, conference room, game room, vending area, computer lab, and a boys & girls club satellite. It is the first to have a boys & girls club satellite center and a computer lab. M-F 5 AM to 9 PM, Sat 9 AM to 5 PM, and Sun 1 PM to 5 PM.

City of Henderson Bird Viewing Preserve and Water Reclamation Facility
2400 Moser Drive
Henderson, NV
OPEN DAILY from 6:00 AM to 3:00 PM.

For mapped trails and several observation stations with benches and signs.

SUMMERLIN

The Trails Park

A 28-acre linear park in The Trails Village. The Trails Park includes three lighted baseball fields, a community center and swimming pool, a children's play area, a meadow area and numerous picnic ramadas.

The Arbors Sports Park

A 60-acre joint-use facility designed and constructed by the City of Las Vegas, Clark County School District and The Howard Hughes Corporation. The park incorporates the 42-acre campus of Palo Verde High School and an 18-acre sports complex. The complex features include an Olympic-size swimming pool, locker facilities, children's play area, picnic area, soccer field and two additional softball fields. The sports complex complements the facilities and amenities available at the high school, which include a football field, soccer field, baseball field, eight tennis courts and six outdoor basketball courts. Plus a 40,000-square-foot community center that will house a full-size gymnasium, shower and locker facilities and meeting and programming rooms.

The Gardens Park and Recreational Center

The center is located on 20.6 acres in The Gardens Village—a large oval shaped park with a variety of distinctive uses including an active recreational area with basketball and tennis courts and Summerlin's first roller hockey rink and rollerblade area; a community center with gardens, bocce, horseshoe and shuffleboard courts; and a large open festival lawn area.

North Las Vegas Recreation Center
1638 N. Bruce Street
North Las Vegas, NV 89030
(702) 633-1600

The recreation center serves the entire City of North Las Vegas offering a myriad of programs for tots, teens, adults, and seniors. The center is open six days a week. In addition, the center offers outdoor swimming programs throughout the summer months at the city's three municipal pools. M-Th 9 AM to 9 PM, Fri 9 AM to 6 PM, and Sat 9 AM to 5 PM.

Appendix

Outdoor Connections

Biking

Escape Mountain Bike Adventures

Escape Mountain Bike Adventures, 8221 W. Charleston Blvd., offers bike tours of Red Rock Canyon. Rental bikes are available. For more information, call 596-2953, check www.escapeadventures.com or send e-mail to bike@escapeadventures.com.

Las Vegas Valley Bicycle Club

The Las Vegas Valley Bicycle Club hosts weekly rides (897-7800).

Las Vegas Wheelmen

The Las Vegas Wheelmen Web site, http://communities.msn.com/LasVegasWheelmen, lists weekly ride schedules, events and cycling news links.

Nellis BMX

The Nellis BMX Track holds weekly BMX racing for all ages every Saturday (453-1663 or 452-6053).

Hikes

Hiking Las Vegas

A 700-page Web site, www.hikinglasvegas.com, has everything you need to know about hiking in Southern Nevada, including trail and route descriptions, photos of all major peaks, enhanced topographical maps and safety tips.

Las Vegas Mountaineers Club

The Las Vegas Mountaineers Club features monthly outings in hiking, backpacking and climbing from the beginner to the advanced. Outings include hiking to peaks such as Charleston Peak and Mummy Mountain in Kyle Canyon, and Bridge Mountain and Turtlehead Peak in Red Rock Canyon. Trip destinations include the Sierras, Utah, Death Valley and Northern Nevada. Training is available to members for all activities. Check www.lvmc.org for information.

Trailblazers Singles Hiking Group

The Trailblazers Singles Hiking Group, for singles in their 30s and 40s, organizes hikes and outdoor activities in the Las Vegas area. For more information visit www.lvtrailblazers.org.

Wilderness Women's Hiking Club

The Wilderness Women's Hiking Club is for women who enjoy the outdoors. Beginners are welcome. For more information, call 392-7327.

Racing

Desert Dash

Desert Dash runs an adventure race series and a mountain bike series in Las Vegas. Adventure racing features three- to five-hour non-motorized off-road races with teams of three or four. The mountain bike series consists of three races with points champions crowned at the end. The races are designed for both the weekend warrior and the elite racer (431-4858, www.desertdash.com).

Running

Las Vegas Hash House Harriers

The Las Vegas Hash House Harriers group schedules noncompetitive cross-country running, jogging and walking for those 21 and older. Meetings are held in various terrains around the Las Vegas Valley (390-4274).

Las Vegas Running Team

The Las Vegas Running Team offers free training runs at 6 PM Mondays-Fridays from various locations throughout the Las Vegas Valley as well as a five- to 20-mile training runs at 6 AM Sundays from Vegas Pointe Plaza, 9155 Las Vegas Blvd. South (450-4788, www.lasvegasrunningteam.com).

Las Vegas Track Club

The Las Vegas Track Club holds races and fun runs each Saturday morning at locations throughout the valley. Organized runs are also held at different locations during the week. Call the runners' hot line at 594-0970 for Saturday events or check www.lvtc.org.

Guided tours

Adventure Las Vegas Tours

Adventure Las Vegas Tours offers 100 different Las Vegas-area tours including horseback riding, ATV, kayak and wakeboarding (938-8687 or 877-486-8758).

All Las Vegas Tours

All Las Vegas Tours offers half- or full-day adventure and sightseeing trips, tours and activities in and around Las Vegas, the Grand Canyon, Hoover Dam and Death Valley. Included are white-water rafting trips; off-road Humvee tours; and glider, airplane and helicopter flights. Personalized nature tours, sky diving, horseback riding, karting and lake cruises are offered also (233-1627, www.alllasvegas-tours.com).

Adventure Photo Tours Inc.

Adventure Photo Tours Inc. offers half-day and full-day tours to Red Rock Canyon National Conservation Area, the Joshua tree forest in the Spring Mountains and the Goodsprings Valley ghost mines. Full-day tours are offered to Valley of Fire, Eldorado Canyon abandoned mines and Logan Wash (889-8687).

American Adventure Tours Inc.

American Adventure Tours Inc. offers a variety of tours including the Grand Canyon; the Colorado River; Moab, Utah; Lake Mead; and Lake Powell. Tours range from half-day to 14-day excursions including ATV, Jeep, mountain bike, horseback riding, hiking, backpacking, watercraft, snowmobile, white-water rafting, float trips and a thrill ride tour that includes roller coasters, bungee jumping, slingshot and the world's tallest zero gravity ride (876-4600, www.americanadventuretours.com).

Ancient Wisdom Tours

Ancient Wisdom Tours, in Kanab, Utah, offers survival skills instruction and wilderness adventure tours. Call (435) 635-0709 for information.

Anglers Edge Guide Service

Anglers Edge Guide Service offers guided fishing

trips for stripers and largemouth bass on Lake Mead and Lake Mojave, and provides all necessary equipment. (285-2814, www.fishanglersedge.com).

Annie Bananie's Wild West Tours

Annie Bananie's Wild West Tours offers a 6 1/2-hour bus tour of Lake Mead National Recreation Area and Valley of Fire. Lunch is included as well as hotel pickup, a guide and a stop at a natural desert oasis (804-9755).

ATV Action Tours Inc.

ATV Action Tours Inc. offers a variety of scenic land tours via off-road vehicles, white-water river rafting and Sea-Doo personal watercraft adventures (566-7400 or 888-288-5200).

Beyond Las Vegas

Beyond Las Vegas offers adventure and learning experiences. Go horseback riding in Red Rock Canyon, see the Grand Canyon by helicopter, drive an ATV quad in the sand or learn about the American Indian history of the Las Vegas area (888-846-4747).

Black Canyon/Willow Beach River Adventures

Black Canyon/Willow Beach River Adventures provides the smooth-water float trip from Hoover Dam to Willow Beach Marina on the Colorado River, south of Hoover Dam (294-1414).

Blindfold Tours & Guide Service Inc.

Blindfold Tours & Guide Service Inc. offers guided four-wheel-drive tours around the Kanab, Utah, area, Bryce Canyon National Park, Zion National Park, the Grand Canyon and the Grand Staircase-Escalante National Monument. Trips range from 1 1/2 hours to all day and include tours to scenic vistas, slot canyons, dinosaur tracks and American Indian rock art. Trips are available for all ages and abilities. Weekend getaway packages are also available. Call (866) 804-1625 toll free for more information.

Colorado River Tours

Colorado River Tours offers 1880 gold mine tours in historic Eldorado Canyon. Visitors may also canoe or kayak at the Blue Water Coves of the Colorado River at the base of the canyon. Shuttles and guides are available (291-0026, 293-4422, www.coloradorivertour.com).

Cowboy Trail Rides

Cowboy Trail Rides offers scenic horseback rides daily at Red Rock Canyon and Kyle Canyon Road on the way to Mount Charleston. A Red Rock sunset dinner ride is held Tuesday through Saturday evenings and features a two-hour rim ride topped with a Western-style barbecue. Wagon rides, seasonal sleigh rides and weddings are also available (387-2457).

Desert Eco-Tours

Desert Eco-Tours offers half- or full-day field trips year-round with trained naturalists to geological or gem collecting sites, ancient American Indian campsites, ghost towns and Area 51. For information, availability or additional membership services, call or visit the nonprofit Nevada Zoological Foundation, 1775 N. Rancho Drive (648-5955, www.lasvegaszoo.org).

Desert Fox Tours

Desert Fox Tours offers three-hour off-road Humvee tours through Red Rock Canyon, including a search for wild mustangs (798-4866).

Drive-Yourself Tours Inc.

Drive-Yourself Tours Inc. offers nine different audiotapes with maps for self-guided tours around Las Vegas and the Grand Canyon. Cassette tapes are $14.95 each (565-8761).

First Travel Tours

First Travel Tours offers a journey to the Grand Canyon in a helicopter via Hoover Dam, Rainbow Canyon, Lake Mead to the West Rim and then down into the Grand Canyon. Then fly to a 105,000-acre ranch for a barbecue lunch. Additional features available include an ATV and horseback guided tours (228-9902).

Fish n Fool Guide Service

Fish n Fool Guide Service offers year-round guided fishing trips to Lake Mead and Lake Mohave. All tackle and refreshments are provided (614-8117, www.fish-n-fool.com).

Hike This!

Hike This! offers single-day guided hiking tours in Red Rock Canyon for fitness and exercise. Call 393-4453 for further information (www.hikethislasvegas.com).

Jackson Hole Mountain Guides and Climbing Schools

Jackson Hole Mountain Guides and Climbing Schools offers one-day guided hikes or scrambles; one-day guided technical climbs; and basic, intermediate and advanced climbing courses in Red Rock Canyon (800-239-7642 or 254-0885).

Lake Mead Cruises

Lake Mead Cruises offers the Eco-Adventure Tour aboard the Velocity. Experience the scenery of Lake Mead National Recreation Area and the Colorado River to the edge of the Grand Canyon on this six-hour cruise (293-6180, www.lakemeadcruises.com).

Leo's Big Bus Senior Tours

Leo's Big Bus Senior Tours features a variety of tours available to senior citizens. Call 645-4289 for information and reservations.

#1 Las Vegas Tours

#1 Las Vegas Tours offers a selection of adventure and sightseeing tours from Las Vegas to Grand Canyon, Hoover Dam, Lake Mead, Death Valley, Red Rock Canyon, Eldorado Canyon and Joshua Tree forests. Try personal watercrafts, white-water rafting, horseback riding, helicopter and plane flights, bus and off-road Jeep tours, all-terrain vehicles, kayaking and lake cruises (toll free 888-609-5665, www.1-las-vegas.com).

Outdoor Source Flyfishers

Outdoor Source Flyfishers is a guided fly-fishing service in the Las Vegas and southern Utah area. Fly-fishing lessons are available for the novice. Group, family and club picnics and company retreats are also offered. For information and options, call 499-8921 or visit our site at: www.outdoorsource.net.

Pink Jeep Tours-Las Vegas Inc.

Pink Jeep Tours-Las Vegas Inc. offers professionally guided sightseeing tours in luxurious, custom Jeeps and sports utility vehicles (895-6777, 888-900-4480, www.pinkjeep.com).

Rebel Adventure Tours

Rebel Adventure Tours offers Jet Skis, white-water rafting, mountain biking, helicopters, sailplanes, gold mining, ATVs, customized Hummers and horseback riding (380-6969).

Red Rock Downhill Bike and Hike

Red Rock Downhill Bike and Hike Tours offers guided tours of Red Rock Canyon and the Valley of Fire (617-8965).

Rocky Trails Inc.

Rocky Trails Inc. offers nature-oriented day trips to Valley of Fire, Red Rock Canyon, Death Valley, Zion National Park and the Grand Canyon (869-9991).

Sagebrush Ranch Trail Rides

Sagebrush Ranch offers a variety of trail rides including a mountain range breakfast ride and sunset steak dinner ride. Children and novice riders are welcome. Lessons and daily rides are available. Call Mary, 655-7991, or Jacque, 645-9422, for information.

Showtime Tours

Showtime Tours offers sightseeing experiences ranging from half-day to full-day tours featuring the Hoover Dam, Lake Mead, the Grand Canyon, river raft floats, Laughlin, ghost mines/ATV excursions, and day and night city tours of Las Vegas (895-9976, www.lasvegastours.com).

Silver State "Old West" Tours

Silver State "Old West" Tours, located in Spring Mountain Ranch State Park, offers scenic horseback trail rides in Red Rock Canyon. Trail rides, stagecoach and wagon rides, Western barbecue events and roping contests are available seven days a week (798-7788).

Sky's The Limit

Sky's The Limit, Nevada's original climbing school, indoor climbing center and mountain guide service, features AMGA accreditation and certified guides, daily entry level through advanced rock craft classes conducted inside the climbing center and at Red Rock, Mount Charleston and the Sierra Nevada. Groups and families are welcome (363-4533, 800-733-7597, www.skysthelimit.com).

Walking Tours

These 1/4-mile, 45-minute daily tours at Spring Mountain Ranch State Park lead to the 1860s blacksmith's shop, the second oldest building in the Las Vegas Valley, and Lake Harriet (875-4141).

Other activities

Adventure Las Vegas

Adventure Las Vegas provides daily scuba, snorkel or hiking trips to Lake Mead on chartered U.S. Coast Guard-approved dive vessels. Half-day and full-day trips are available (938-8687 or 877-486-8758).

The Adventurers

The Adventurers group offers activities from dinners and parties to river rafting and weekend getaways to places like Catalina Island, for those looking to meet people between the ages of 20s and 50s (650-2629, www.LasVegasAdventurers.com).

The Adventurers are planning a trip for whitewater rafting on the American River in Northern California July 19-21. Call 650-2629 for more information.

Alpine Ski & Snowboard Club

The Alpine Ski & Snowboard Club provides winter sports, travel and social events for Las Vegas adults and organizes trips throughout the United States and Europe. In addition, the club holds parties from 7 to 10 PM Thursdays at Roadrunner Casino Las Vegas, 2839 W. Sahara Ave. (227-8787).

Around the Bend Friends

Around the Bend Friends, a group for those over 50 interested in outdoor activities, meets at 6 PM the second Tuesday of the month in the Dula Gymnasium, 441 E. Bonanza Road. Call 877-6296 for more information.

Balloon Las Vegas

Balloon Las Vegas offers sunrise and sunset hot-air balloon flights daily, including a three-hour trip from the Strip, champagne celebrations and weddings with all the options. Family and group rates are available. Call 596-7582 for more information.

Clark County Parks and Recreation

Clark County Parks and Recreation offers a variety

of classes including backpacking and camping skills, desert survival, fossil hunting, gold prospecting, hiking and rock climbing. There are also adventure outings in Arizona, Utah and throughout Southern Nevada. Call 455-8289 for further information.

The Dunes and Trails ATV Club

The Dunes and Trails ATV Club meets at 7:30 PM the second Thursday of each month at The Tap House, 5589 W. Charleston Blvd. The club offers trail and dune rides twice each month for ATV riders of all skill levels. In addition, the club is involved with rider education, resource protection and establishing riding opportunities (270-3750, www.dunesandtrailsatv.org).

Eldorado Cowboys Single Action Shooting Society

The Eldorado Cowboys Single Action Shooting Society meets the first Sunday of each month at Jean. The main match starts at 8 AM. Long range will start immediately after the main stages are completed. The group promotes the western cowboy action shooting fantasy. Visitors are welcome (565-3736, www.nevadacas.com).

Lake Mead Boat Owners Association

The Lake Mead Boat Owners Association is dedicated to promoting the safety, welfare and enjoyment of all users of Lake Mead. The association meets at 10 AM the third Sunday of the month at

Lake Mead Marina. Boaters and nonboaters are welcome (294-1185).

Las Vegas Fly-Fishing Club

The Las Vegas Fly-Fishing Club meets at 7 PM the third Tuesday of each month at the O.C. Lee Building, 1250 S. Burnham St. The group participates in conservation work, education, outings, awards and raffles.

Las Vegas GravityZone Sky Diving Center

Las Vegas GravityZone Sky Diving Center invites beginners and advanced sky divers to experience tandem skydiving and accelerated free fall. Videos and pictures are available (612-8221).

Las Vegas Ski & Sports Club

The Las Vegas Ski & Sports Club offers downhill and cross-country ski trips, hiking, canoeing, river rafting, tennis, camping, boating and other sporting events. TGIF is held at 6 PM the second and fourth Friday of each month at various locations (458-0469, www.lasvegasskiclub.com).

Las Vegas Soaring Center

The Las Vegas Soaring Center offers one- and two-passenger rides in a high-performance sailplane or in the open cockpit of a biplane (874-1010).

Loners on Wheels

Loners on Wheels is a national singles RV organization. The Las Vegas chapter meets the third

Thursday of every month except June, July, August and December. Call 873-3079 for further information.

Nevada Striper Fishing Club

The Nevada Striper Fishing Club hosts weekend striper fishing tournaments as well as an annual day of fishing for disabled and disadvantaged children. The group meets at 7:30 PM the second Thursday of each month at Lake Mead Lounge & Casino, 846 E. Lake Mead Drive, Henderson (565-8183).

Powerhouse Climbing Center

The Powerhouse Climbing Center offers 8,000 square feet of textured climbing terrain (254-5604).

Quail Unlimited

The Southern Nevada Chapter of Quail Unlimited meets at 7 PM the fourth Tuesday of each month at the O.C. Lee Building, 1250 S. Burnham St. The group is open to those interested in upland wildlife. Volunteers develop and restore habitat for quail, dove, chukar, grouse, pheasant and turkey. Call 528-5808 for further information.

Sailing Ventures of Nevada

Sailing Ventures of Nevada, a professional training facility, offers comprehensive classes for American Sailing Association certification. Beginning and intermediate classes are offered at Lake Mead (877-542-1691, www.sailingventures.com).

Skydive Las Vegas

Boulder City's Skydive Las Vegas offers instruction and skydiving for beginner and advanced sky divers (293-1860).

Southern Nevada Paddling Club

The Southern Nevada Paddling Club, for people who have an interest in kayaking, offers day and overnight trips on Lake Mead and the Colorado River. Meetings are held the first Wednesday of each month (www.kayaknevada.org).

Thrillseekers Unlimited

Thrillseekers Unlimited, owned and operated by athletes and stunt professionals, offers various vacation and weekend packages featuring adventures such as fire walking; paragliding; bungee jumping; rock climbing/rappelling; indoor and tandem skydiving; and snowboarding or mountain boarding, depending on the season (699-5550, www.ThrillseekersUnlimited.com).

Trout Unlimited

The Southern Nevada Chapter of Trout Unlimited meets at 7 PM the first Thursday of each month at 4747 Vegas Drive. The group is involved in many conservation projects and offers several trips through the year. Meetings include a program and raffle. Call 497-9396 for more information.

Wildlife and Habitat Improvement of Nevada

Wildlife and Habitat Improvement of Nevada meets at 7 PM each fourth Tuesday at the O.C. Lee Building, 1250 S. Burnham. This is a local nonprofit group supporting conservation projects in Nevada for its wildlife and wildlife habitat. For more information write Wildlife and Habitat Improvement of Nevada, P.O. Box 98435, Las Vegas, NV 89193-8435.

Wilderness Volunteers

Wilderness Volunteers is a nonprofit organization that works in cooperation with public land agencies to organize trips that combine adventure and travel with an opportunity for participants to become stewards of America's wild lands. For more information, call toll free (888) 737-2888 or visit www.wildernessvolunteers.org.

*   *   *

Information provided by Jean Bard of the Las Vegas Review-Journal. *For updated listings, consult the newspaper's website, lvrj.com.*

Appendix

Clubs and Organizations

VETERANS ASSOCIATION

The Silver State Basha chapter of the China-Burma-India Veterans Association holds monthly luncheon meetings (382-9638 or 457-2617).

BRIDGE CLUB

Bridge World II meets at 1 PM Mondays, Wednesdays, Thursdays, Fridays and Saturdays for duplicate bridge at Charleston Heights Arts Center, 800 S. Brush St. An open game is held Thursdays at 6 PM at West Flamingo Active Adult Center, 6255 W. Flamingo Road (735-3114).

TRAVEL CLUB

The Singles Travel Club, a group that plans local and world travels, meets at 6 PM every second and fourth Monday at the Tap House, 5589 W. Charleston Blvd. (650-8564).

JAPANESE AMERICAN LEAGUE

The Japanese American Citizens League will hold a general monthly meeting at 7 PM Monday at Nevada Power Co., 6226 W. Sahara Ave. (382-4443).

COMMUNITY CLASSES

The Las Vegas Department of Leisure Services holds community classes throughout the week at different times and locations. Call 229-6720 for details.

ADVENTURE CLUB

The Adventurers—a group interested in river rafting, hot-air ballooning, hiking, skydiving and other activities—holds several monthly activities. Sand volleyball games are held at 7 PM Wednesdays at Sunset Park, 2601 E. Sunset Road. For more information and upcoming events, call 650-2629.

CANCER SCREENINGS

Women's Health Connection offers free breast and cervical cancer screenings to uninsured and under-insured women, ages 40 to 64. Women 50 and older also will get mammograms. Women younger than 50 will get mammograms if screenings indicate the need. Call 212-6381 for details. St. Rose Dominican Hospital offers free breast cancer screenings and services to uninsured and underinsured women, ages 40 and younger. Call 616-7525 for qualifying information.

The American Cancer Society and Sunrise Hospital and Medical Center are offering $56 mammograms through the end of the year. Call (800) 227-2345 to schedule an appointment.

SOCIAL CLUB

A Southern Highlands Community Singles Group is forming. Call 378-9900 for more information.

This information was provided courtesy of Ronelle Botwinik of the Las Vegas Review-Journal. *An updated version of this list can be found on the web at lvrj.com.*

Appendix

Bowling Lanes

Boulder Bowl
504 California Ave.
Boulder City
(702) 293-2368

Castaways Hotel Casino & Bowling Center
(Formerly Showboat)
2800 Fremont St.
(702) 385-9153

Gold Coast Hotel & Casino
4000 W. Flamingo Road
(702) 367-4700

Sunset Lanes
4451 E. Sunset Rd.
(between Green Valley Pkwy & Mountain Vista)
(702) 736-BOWL (2695)

Mahoney's Silver Nugget Bowling Center
2140 Las Vegas Blvd. North
(702) 320-BOWL (2695)

Orleans Hotel & Casino
4500 W. Tropicana Ave
(702) 365-7400

Sam's Town Hotel Bowling Center
5111 Boulder Hwy. (at Flamingo Road)
(702) 454-8022

Sante Fe Station
4949 N. Rancho Drive
(702) 658-4900

Suncoast Hotel & Casino
9090 Alta Drive
(702) 636-7400

Terrible's Town Casino & Bowl
642 S. Boulder Hwy
(702) 564-7118

Texas Station Gambling Hall & Hotel
2101 Texas Star Lane
(at Lake Mead Blvd. and Rancho Drive)
(702) 631-1000

Appendix

Fitness and Exercise Centers

24 HOUR FITNESS

Features free weights and a wide array of cardiovascular machines and fitness equipment, plus programs for diet, fitness, and weight control.

> 3055 S. Valley View Blvd.
> (702) 368-1111
>
> 4480 E. Charleston Blvd.
> (702) 459-4241
>
> 3141 N. Rainbow Blvd.
> (702) 656-7777
>
> 2605 S. Eastern Ave.
> (702) 641-2222

APOLLO SPA & HEALTH CLUB

953 E. Sahara Ave.
(702) 650-9191

BETTER BODIES NUTRITION

Programs for personal care & beauty, diet, fitness
and weight control. Personal trainers available.
2230 N. Rainbow Blvd.
(702) 631-3000

BODY BEAUTIFUL TAN & TONE

6400 S. Eastern Ave.
(702) 736-2264

CHUCK MINKER SPORTS COMPLEX

A sports facility with indoor racquetball courts.
275 North Mojave
(702) 229-6563

COMFORT ZONE

Sports & recreation facility with personal trainers.
3131 Industrial Road
(702) 312-5400

CURTIS' BODY SHOP

4040 Industrial Rd.
(702) 696-9292

DEDICATION PERSONAL TRAINING

Sports & recreation facility with personal trainers.
2900 E. Patrick Lane, Suite 4B
(702) 795-8282

FOR WOMEN ONLY FITNESS CENTER

Fitness center for women.
1142 S. Rainbow Blvd.
(702) 258-1226

FUN 'N FITNESS

2520 S Eastern Ave.
(702) 431-7667

GOLD'S GYM

Offers a variety of body-sculpting fitness programs
and diet planning.

4720 West Sahara Ave.
(702) 877-6966

3750 E. Flamingo Road
(702) 451-4222

7501 W. Lake Mead Blvd.
(702) 360-8205

GREEN VALLEY ATHLETIC CLUB

2100 Olympic Ave. in Henderson
(702) 454-6000

HATHA YOGA CENTER

Sports & recreation center with Yoga.
7260 W. Lake Mead Blvd., Suite 3
(702) 233-9042

JUDY GILLETTE'S FOR WOMEN ONLY FITNESS CENTER

4451 E. Sunset Road
(702) 898-7972

LAS VEGAS ATHLETIC CLUBS

Sports and recreation centers with racquetball courts.

Corporate Headquarters
2655 S. Maryland Parkway, STE 201
Las Vegas, NV 89109-1666
(702) 734-8944

5200 W. Sahara Ave
(702) 734-5822
(702) 364-5822

3830 E. Flamingo Road
(702) 898-5822

5090 S. Maryland Parkway
(702) 795-2582

2655 S. Maryland Parkway
(702) 734-5822

LAS VEGAS SPORTING HOUSE

Offers personal care & beauty and health & alternative medicine programs, plus racquetball courts.
3025 Industrial Road
(702) 733-8999

MEDINA'S FITNESS CENTER

133 S. Water St. in Henderson
(702) 564-7377

PLATINUM FITNESS

3135 Industrial Rd.
(702) 791-1901

Q THE SPORTS CLUB

601 S. Rainbow Blvd.
(702) 258-7080

SUNRISE FITNESS CENTER

4480 E. Charleston Blvd.
(702) 459-4241

THE SPORTS CLUB

Sports and recreation center with racquetball courts.
5020 E. Tropicana Ave.
(702) 547-6400

UNIVERSITY OF NEVADA, LAS VEGAS

Sports complex and racquetball courts.
4505 S. Maryland Parkway
(702) 895-3150

YMCA SPORTS COMPLEX AND RACQUETBALL COURTS WITH SWIMMING

4141 Meadows Lane
(702) 877-9622

657 Town Center Drive
(702) 240-9622

3521 N. Durango Drive
(702) 240-9622

List courtesy of the Las Vegas Review-Journal. *An updated version of this list can be found on the Web at lvrj.com.*

Appendix

Swimming Pools

City of Las Vegas

Baker Swimming Pool
1100 E. St. Louis Ave.
(702) 229-6395
Hours: 1-4:45 PM Monday-Friday; noon-4:45 PM
Saturday

Brinley Swimming Pool
2480 Maverick St.
(702) 799-6784
Hours: 1-4:45 PM Monday-Friday; noon-4:45 PM
Saturday

Cragin Swimming Pool
900 Hinson St.
(702) 229-6394
Hours: 1-4:45 PM Monday, Wednesday and Friday; 10-4:45 PM Tuesday and Thursday; and noon-4:45 PM Saturday

Doolittle Swimming Pool
1901 N. J St.
(702) 229-6398
Hours: 9:30-11 AM and 1-4:45 PM Monday, Wednesday and Friday; 11 AM to 4:45 PM Tuesday and Thursday; and noon-4:45 PM Saturday

Garside Swimming Pool
300 S. Torrey Pines Drive
(702) 229-6393
Hours: 1-4:45 PM Monday-Friday; noon-4:45 PM Saturday; 7-9 PM Monday, Wednesday and Friday; and 5:30-6:30 PM Tuesday through Thursday

Hadland Swimming Pool
2800 E. Stewart Ave.
(702) 229-6397
Hours: 1-4:45 PM Monday, Wednesday and Friday; 10 AM to 4:45 PM Tuesday through Thursday; and noon-4:45 PM Saturday

Municipal Pool
431 E. Bonanza Road
(702) 229-6309
Hours: 8 AM to 9 PM Mondays-Friday; 9 AM to 6 PM Saturday; 11 AM to 5 PM Sunday

Trails Swimming Pool
1920 Spring Gate Lane
(702) 229-4629
Hours: 1-4:45 PM Monday-Friday; noon-4:45 PM
Saturday; 7-9 PM Monday, Wednesday and Friday;
and 5:30-6:30 PM Tuesday through Thursday

Pool Fees: Free for children ages 0-3
$1 ages 4-17
$2 ages 18-54
$1.50 for ages 55 and above
Season passes also available

Clark County

Pools operated by the Clark County Department of
Parks and Recreation are open June 5-Aug. 20. The
pools at Sunset and Sunrise parks are also open for
Memorial Day weekend and the last weekend of
August and first weekend of September.

Desert Breeze Indoor Pool (open year-round)
8275 W. Spring Mountain Road
(702) 455-7798
Hours: Open Swim: 1-4 PM Monday-Friday; 7-9:30
PM Monday, Wednesday, Friday; 11 AM to 6 PM
Saturday & Sunday. Lap Swimming: 6 AM to 1 PM
and 7:30-9:30 PM Monday-Friday; 9 AM to 6 PM
Saturday; 11 AM to 6 PM Sunday. At least one lane is
always available.

Desert Inn Pool
3570 Vista Del Monte
(702) 455-7531
Hours: 1-5 PM Monday, Wednesday, Friday and
Sunday; 1-6:30 PM Tuesday and Thursday; and
noon-5 PM Saturday.

Maslow Park
4902 Lana Drive
(702) 455-8540
Hours: 1-5 PM Monday-Friday; 11 AM to 5 PM
Saturday; and noon-5 PM Sunday.

Parkdale Park
3200 Ferndale St.
(702) 455-7523
Hours: 1-5 PM Monday-Friday; 11 AM to 5 PM
Saturday; and noon-5 PM Sunday.

Sunrise Park
2240 Linn Lane
(702) 455-7610
Hours: 1:30-5 PM Monday-Friday; 11 AM to 5 PM
Saturday; and noon-5 PM Sunday.

Sunset Park and Lake
2601 E. Sunset Road
(702) 455-8225
Hours: 1-5 PM Monday-Friday; 11 AM to 5 PM
Saturday; and noon-5 PM Sunday.

Von Tobel Community Center
3610 E. Carey Ave.
(702) 455-7625
Hours: 3:30-6:30 PM Monday-Friday; 10 AM to 6 PM Saturday; and 11 AM to 6 PM Sunday.

Whitney Park
5700 Missouri Ave.
(702) 455-8529
Hours: 1:30-5 PM Monday-Friday; 11 AM to 5 PM Saturday; and noon-5 PM Sunday.

Appendix

Support Groups

SUPPORT GROUPS

The Las Vegas chapter of Children and Adults with Attention Deficit Disorder will meet at 6 PM Monday at Clark County Library, 1401 E. Flamingo Road (363-4776 or 434-7913).

Lake Mead Hospital offers an eating disorders support group at 6 PM Mondays at 1409 E. Lake Mead Blvd., North Las Vegas (822-1188).

International Church of Las Vegas holds a Road to Recovery support group at 7 PM Mondays at 8100 Westcliff Drive (680-0731).

The We Can Make It Family Group of Al-Anon, a support group for families and friends of alcoholics, meets at 1 PM Mondays at First Christian Church, 101 S. Rancho Drive, Room 6 (459-4341 or 341-6729).

Al-Anon holds nonsmoking meetings, "How It Works," at 3:30 PM Mondays, and "From Survival to Recovery" at 3:30 PM Wednesdays at Christ Episcopal Church, 2000 S. Maryland Parkway, Room 1 (388-0644).

A support group for those co-infected with HIV and hepatitis C is held at 5:30 PM Mondays at UMC Wellness Center, 2300 S. Rancho Drive, Suite 205 (384-9104).

The Anger Management Support Group meets at 6:30 PM Mondays at Central Christian Church, 1001 New Beginnings Drive, Henderson, Room 227 (735-4004, Ext. 224).

Calvary Community Assembly of God, 2900 N. Torrey Pines Drive, holds Celebrate Recovery and Divorce Care support groups at 6:30 PM Mondays (656-2900).

An open Grief Support Group meets at 6:30 PM Mondays at Green Valley Presbyterian Church, 1798 Wigwam Parkway, Henderson (564-9797).

Divorced & Widowed Adjustment Inc. offers free support programs Mondays, Wednesdays and

Thursdays. Call 735-5544 for a schedule of times and locations.

Healing the Emotions of Your Divorce recovery program is held Mondays, Tuesdays and Thursdays at Canyon Ridge Christian Church, 6200 W. Lone Mountain Road. Call 656-1272 for details.

Community Action Against Rape and Safe House offer Circle of Friends, a support group for survivors of sexual assault, at 6 PM Mondays. Call 385-2153 for location.

Resolve of Southern Nevada holds peer and professionally led groups for infertility support. Call 392-1770 for details.

Narcotics Anonymous holds weekly support group meetings. Call 369-3362 for times and locations.

The Better Breathers Club, sponsored by the American Lung Association, meets at several locations. Call 431-6333 for details.

Take Off Pounds Sensibly is a nonprofit organization that offers support to those trying to lose weight. For the nearest TOPS chapter in Clark County, call 388-1786.

Overeaters Anonymous, a 12-step program for compulsive eaters, holds meetings throughout the week. Call 593-2945 for times and locations.

Compulsive Eaters Anonymous, a 12-step program for anyone with a desire to stop eating compulsively, meets daily at various times and locations (393-6570).

The Society of Widowed Persons of Southern Nevada holds monthly meetings. Call 453-0800 for complete schedule.

Recovery Inc., a self-help support group for those with overwhelming stress, nervous tension, sleep problems, worry, depression, anger, guilt, fear, anxiety, panic and other emotional problems, meets weekly at four locations. Call 362-7368 for details.

Chapter 277 of Mended Hearts Inc. is a support group for people who have had heart disease and their families. Call 869-9531 for meeting times and locations.

This information was provided courtesy of Ronelle Botwinik of the Las Vegas Review-Journal. *An updated version of this list can be found on the Web at lvrj.com.*

Appendix

Senior Activities

BOULDER CITY CENTER

The Boulder City Center, 1001 Arizona St., offers a 50-cent continental breakfast, weekday buffet-style lunch with a full salad bar for $1.50, Meals on Wheels, door-to-door transportation for $1 per ride (7:30 AM to 10 PM daily), live entertainment, exercise classes, yoga, Wednesday Morning Health Fair, billiards, bingo, cards and silk flower arranging, (293-3320).

CAMBEIRO CENTER

The Arturo Cambeiro Senior Center, 330 N. 13th St., is open 9 AM to 4 PM Mondays through Fridays.

It is managed by the Nevada Association of Latin Americans. Spanish and English are spoken (382-6252, Ext. 135). Meals are served to people ages 60 and older at 11:30 AM daily for a donation of $1.50.

The center also offers classes in citizenship and conversational English, arts and crafts, exercise programs, folkloric dances and table games.

CAMBRIDGE CENTER

Cambridge Center, 3930 Cambridge St., offers a meal program on Fridays for $1.50. Preregistration is recommended (455-7169).

Activities at the center include bingo, field trips and guest speakers. The Clark County Health District conducts blood-pressure checkups 9:30-11:30 AM the second Friday of each month.

CORA COLEMAN SENIOR CENTER

The Cora Coleman Senior Center, 2100 Bonnie Lane, is open 9 AM to 6 PM Mondays through Fridays (455-7617).

Classes offered include arts and crafts, computer skills, defensive driving, exercise and dance, and special-interest courses. Other activities include card games, health screenings, guest speakers and holiday celebrations.

Field trips to various natural and man-made attractions in Southern Nevada are scheduled throughout the year.

DERFELT CENTER

The Derfelt Center in Lorenzi Park, 3333 W.

Washington Ave., offers activities 8 AM to 4 PM Mondays through Fridays for people ages 55 and older (229-6601).

Take Off Pounds Sensibly meets at 9 AM Thursdays. Other activities and classes include arts and crafts; quilting, knitting and sewing; creative writing; bridge; mah-jongg; ballroom, tap and line dancing; yoga; tai chi; sign language; and Spanish.

DOOLITTLE SENIOR CENTER

Doolittle Satellite Senior Center, 1940 N. J St., is open 8:30 AM to 5 PM Mondays through Fridays (229-6125).

The Senior Nutrition Program serves lunch at 11:30 AM Mondays through Fridays for a donation of $1.75.

The center also offers bingo, bowling, table tennis, chair exercise classes, crafts, line dancing, sewing, monthly birthday parties and a community garden project.

DULA GYMNASIUM

Dula Gymnasium, 441 E. Bonanza Road, adjacent to the Las Vegas Senior Citizens Center, offers a variety of classes and activities such as basketball, a walking group, weight-loss classes, bridge and pinochle, tap instruction, table and paddle tennis, tai chi and cribbage (229-6307).

FRIENDSHIP CIRCLE

Friendship Circle, 830 E. Lake Mead Drive, Henderson, is operated by The Salvation Army.

Hours are 7 AM to 5 PM Mondays through Fridays (565-8836).

Services include the Star Program for physically and mentally disabled adults, meals, nursing, and mental and physical exercise. Low-income assistance and Medicaid are available.

HENDERSON SENIOR CENTER

Henderson Senior Center, 27 E. Texas Ave., is open 8 AM to 10 PM Mondays through Thursdays; 8 AM to 4 PM Fridays; and 8 AM to 2 PM Saturdays and Sundays (565-6990).

Lunch is served 11:30 AM to 12:30 PM Mondays through Fridays for a suggested donation of $1.25. Meals also are delivered (565-4626).

Breakfast is offered 9-11 AM Saturdays. Cost is $1.25. On Sunday, lunch is served at noon for $1.

Classes and activities include arts and crafts, billiards, bingo, knitting and crocheting, line dancing and card games.

Services include blood-pressure screenings, medical forms assistance and Social Security assistance.

HOLLYHOCK CENTER

Hollyhock Adult Day Care Center, 380 N. Maryland Parkway, is operated by the Economic Opportunity Board of Clark County. The center offers programs to meet the needs of elderly and impaired individuals and specializes in the care of Alzheimer's patients (382-0093).

LAS VEGAS SENIOR CITIZENS CENTER

Las Vegas Senior Citizens Center, 451 E. Bonanza Road, is open 9 AM to 10 PM Mondays through Saturdays (229-6454).

Classes and activities include beading and knitting, painting, dancing, pinochle, exercise classes, blood-pressure checks, monthly birthday parties and living will workshops.

Several groups meet at the center each month including Clark County Gem Club; Cactus, Water & Energy Conservation Society; Senior Citizen Originals; Senior Tripsters; Senior Citizen Advisory Board; International Association of Certified Ceramic Duncan Teachers; and the 10th Amendment Club.

The Nevada Humanities Committee and Discussion Group meets 10-11:30 AM Thursdays.

LIED SENIOR CENTER

Lied Senior Care Center, 901 N. Jones Blvd., provides daily supervision of frail and disabled adults. The center, operated by the Economic Opportunity Board of Clark County, offers social activities, individual care, medication supervision, meals, stroke exercise classes and other therapies (648-3425).

MARTIN LUTHER KING SENIOR CENTER

The Economic Opportunity Board of Clark County Senior Center, 2420 N. Martin Luther King Blvd., Suite B, offers social activities, health services,

Spanish and English as a second language classes, computer classes, YMCA fitness programs, a fitness room, bingo and other activities (647-2536).

NORTH LAS VEGAS RECREATION CENTER

North Las Vegas Recreation Center, 1638 Bruce St., offers activities for senior citizens 9 AM to 2 PM Mondays through Fridays (633-1492 or 633-1600).

Classes and activities include gym walking, tai chi, sittercize, beginning computer sessions, ceramics, arts and crafts, bridge, dances, seminars and meal service. Monthly trips also are organized.

NORTHWEST COMMUNITY CENTER

Northwest Community Center, 6841 W. Lone Mountain Road, is the home of the Las Vegas Senior Citizen Outreach Programs office. The office plans and executes programs for senior citizens throughout the community and sponsors the Volunteer Senior Park Ambassador Program (229-4924).

Activities include fitness classes, pancake breakfasts, movies, and hearing and eye screenings. There also is a walking group.

OVERTON SENIOR CENTER

United Seniors Inc., 475 S. Moapa Valley Blvd., Overton, offers senior activities 8 AM to 4 PM Mondays through Fridays (702-397-8002).

Meals are served five days a week for a donation of $2.50. Meals on Wheels also is available for the homebound for a donation of $2.50.

Classes and activities include cards, billiards,

ceramics, line dancing, hearing aid services, blood-pressure checks and medical equipment loans.

PARADISE COMMUNITY CENTER

Paradise Community Center, 4770 S. Harrison Drive, offers senior activities, including movie days, bingo and field trips, 7:30 AM to 7 PM Mondays through Fridays and 9 AM to 4 PM Saturdays (455-7513).

PARKDALE COMMUNITY CENTER

Parkdale Community Center, 3200 Ferndale St., offers activities for senior citizens 8 AM to 5 PM (455-8502).

The center houses a computer lab, arts and crafts area, and multipurpose room. Classes include dance, language, arts and crafts, exercise, computers, finance, and health and nutrition. There also are game days and field trips planned each month.

SILVER MESA RECREATION CENTER

Silver Mesa Recreation Center, 4025 Allen Lane, North Las Vegas, offers activities for senior citizens 9-11:30 AM Mondays through Fridays (633-2550).

Classes and activities include tai chi, yoga, gym walking, chess, checkers, basketball, volleyball, billiards, table tennis, cribbage and others. There also is a fitness room. Monthly senior trips are arranged through the neighborhood recreation center (633-1600).

WEST FLAMINGO ACTIVE ADULT CENTER

West Flamingo Active Adult Center, 6255 W. Flamingo Road, is open 8:15 AM to 5 PM Mondays, Wednesdays and Fridays; 8:15 AM to 9 PM on Tuesdays and Thursdays; and 8:15 AM to 4 PM Saturdays (455-7742). The center is open to those 50 and older.

Activities include acting classes, computer classes, knitting and crocheting, exercise classes, tai chi, yoga, watercolor, dance classes, table tennis, card games, field trips and special events.

WHITNEY SENIOR CENTER

Whitney Senior Center, 5712 Missouri Ave., is open 8 AM to 5 PM Mondays, Thursdays and Fridays and 8 AM to 9 PM Tuesdays and Wednesdays (455-7576).

Classes include art, ceramics, collectibles, computer, defensive driving, exercise, sign language and feng shui. Activities include bingo, cards, guest speakers, holiday celebrations, mah-jongg and field trips, among others.

WINCHESTER COMMUNITY CENTER

Winchester Community Center, 3130 S. McLeod Drive, offers social activities including cards, lectures, movies, field trips, senior exercise, tai chi, oil painting and ceramics. An art gallery and a walking path also are at the center. An open house is held 10 AM to 3 PM Wednesdays. A book club meets at 2 PM the second and fourth Thursday of each month (455-7340).

SENIOR PROGRAMS

The Henderson Allied Community Advocates group offers help to people age 55 and older who need assistance with transportation, Meals on Wheels, respite care and senior companionship (486-6770, Ext. 243).

Senior Class Action Trips, a group for seniors, their families and friends on limited incomes, meets at various times and places. Call 362-5744 for more information.

Seniors on the Go offers short bus trips for senior citizens (656-2982).

The Senior Adventurers Travel Club offers day and extended trips and cruises to senior citizens, their families and friends (247-8780).

The Senior Wheels USA program makes available power wheelchairs to senior citizens and other permanently disabled, at no charge, with qualification (1-800-360-8765).

The Southern Nevada chapter of the Alzheimer's Association offers information about the disease, along with support and other services. Support groups meet at various locations (248-2770).

The Barbara Greenspun WomensCare Center of Excellence holds a breast cancer support group at 6 PM on the second and fourth Monday of each month at St. Rose Dominican Hospital, 100 N. Green Valley Parkway, Suite 30, Henderson (914-7060).

Clark County Health District, 625 Shadow Lane, offers a foot care clinic 8 AM to 4 PM weekdays. Call for an appointment. A donation is requested (383-1331).

The Las Vegas Tappers are looking for men and women to exercise and tap (361-8593).

Information provided by Jean Bard of the Las Vegas Review-Journal. *For updated listings, consult the newspaper's website, lvrj.com.*

Appendix

Housing Appreciation

Home prices in Southern Nevada appreciated an average of five percent in early 2002, according to the *Las Vegas Review-Journal* and SalesTraq, a real estate research firm. The following are the average percentage gains and losses by zip code.

89011	- 1 %
89012	+ 4 %
89014	0
89015	+ 4 %
89030	+ 5 %
89031	+ 8 %
89032	+ 6 %
89052	+ 6 %

89101	+ 3 %
89102	+16 %
89104	+ 6 %
89106	+ 3 %
89107	+10 %
89108	+ 7 %
89109	- 2 %
89110	+ 4 %
89113	+ 8 %
89114	- 5 %
89117	+11 %
89120	+10 %
89121	+ 6 %
89122	+ 7 %
89123	+ 7 %
89124	+10 %
89128	+ 2 %
89129	+ 8 %
89130	+ 7 %
89131	+11 %
89134	+ 3 %
89135	+12 %
89139	- 6 %
89141	0
89143	+17 %
89145	+ 2 %
89146	- 8 %
89148	- 1 %
89149	- 6 %

Appendix

Maps

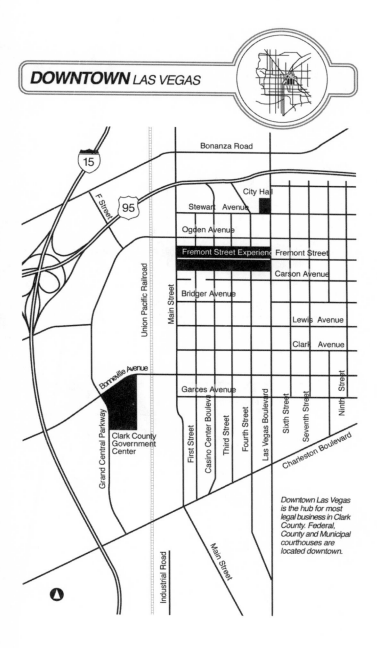

DOWNTOWN LAS VEGAS

Bonanza Road

15

95

F Street

City Hall

Stewart Avenue

Ogden Avenue

Fremont Street Experience Fremont Street

Carson Avenue

Bridger Avenue

Lewis Avenue

Clark Avenue

Union Pacific Railroad

Main Street

Bonneville Avenue

Garces Avenue

First Street

Casino Center Boulevard

Third Street

Fourth Street

Las Vegas Boulevard

Sixth Street

Seventh Street

Ninth Street

Grand Central Parkway

Clark County
Government
Center

Charleston Boulevard

Industrial Road

Main Street

*Downtown Las Vegas
is the hub for most
legal business in Clark
County. Federal,
County and Municipal
courthouses are
located downtown.*

NORTHWEST LAS VEGAS

Kyle Canyon Road
(157)
To Mt. Charleston
95

Grand Teton Drive

Note: Some Northern segments of I-215 (Las Vegas Beltway) are under construction and completion is expected in late 2003.

Durango Drive
Buffalo Drive
Tenaya Way
Rainbow Boulevard
Jones Boulevard
Decatur Boulevard

To I-15

Centennial Parkway

Apache Road
Drive

Ann Road

Lone Mountain Road

Craig Road

Alexander Rd.

Fort
Rampart

Rancho

Cheyenne Ave.

Lake Mead Boulevard

Smoke Ranch Road

Summerlin Pkwy.

Vegas Drive

Washington Avenue

Drive

215
Hualapai Way

95

Charleston Boulevard

To Red Rock Canyon National Recreation Area

Fort Apache Road

Sahara Avenue

Durango Road
Buffalo Drive
Tenaya Way
Rainbow Boulevard
Jones Boulevard
Decatur Boulevard
Valley View Boulevard

15

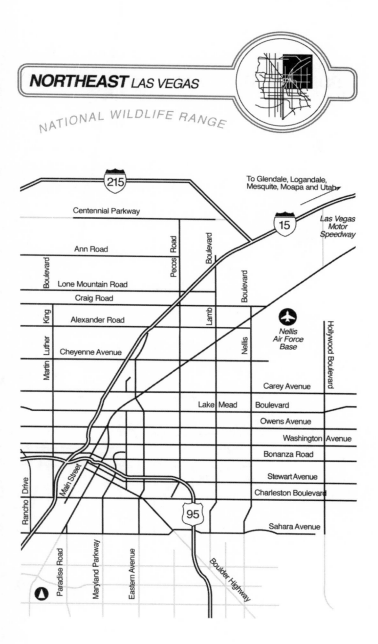

NORTHEAST *LAS VEGAS*

NATIONAL WILDLIFE RANGE

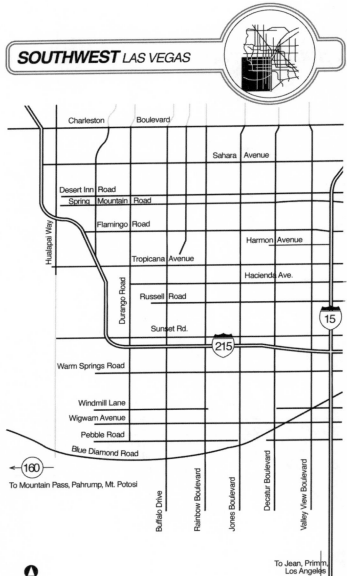

SOUTHWEST LAS VEGAS

Charleston Boulevard

Sahara Avenue

Desert Inn Road

Spring Mountain Road

Flamingo Road

Hualapai Way

Harmon Avenue

Tropicana Avenue

Hacienda Ave.

Durango Road

Russell Road

Sunset Rd.

215

15

Warm Springs Road

Windmill Lane

Wigwam Avenue

Pebble Road

Blue Diamond Road

160

To Mountain Pass, Pahrump, Mt. Potosi

Buffalo Drive

Rainbow Boulevard

Jones Boulevard

Decatur Boulevard

Valley View Boulevard

To Jean, Primm,
Los Angeles

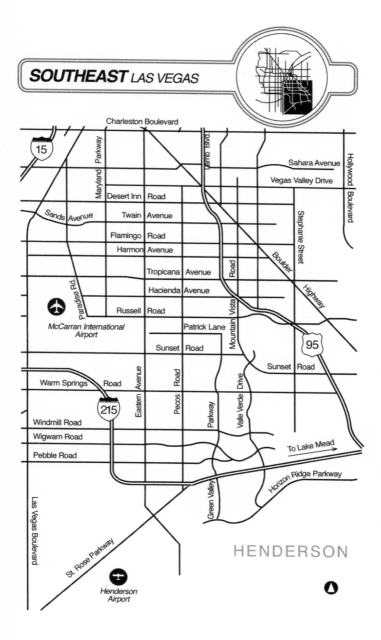

SOUTHEAST *LAS VEGAS*

Charleston Boulevard

15

Maryland Parkway

Lamb Blvd.

Sahara Avenue

Vegas Valley Drive

Hollywood Boulevard

Desert Inn Road

Sands Avenue

Twain Avenue

Flamingo Road

Harmon Avenue

Stephanie Street

Tropicana Avenue

Hacienda Avenue

Russell Road

Road

Boulder

Highway

Paradise Rd.

Patrick Lane

McCarran International
Airport

Sunset Road

Mountain Vista

95

Sunset Road

Warm Springs Road

Eastern Avenue

Pecos Road

Valle Verde Drive

215

Windmill Road

Wigwam Road

Pebble Road

Parkway

To Lake Mead

Horizon Ridge Parkway

Las Vegas Boulevard

St. Rose Parkway

Green Valley

HENDERSON

Henderson
Airport

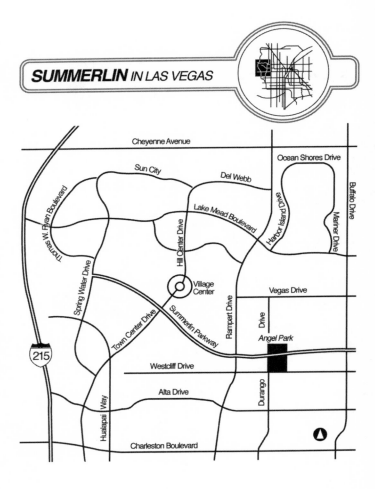

SUMMERLIN *IN LAS VEGAS*

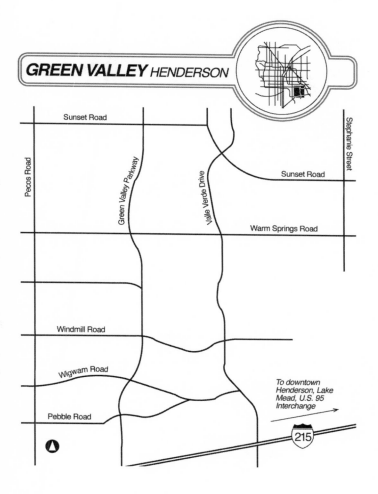

Index

292